Mohit Arora

Embedded System Design

Introduction to SoC System Architecture

Learning Bytes
—PUBLISHING—

Mohit Arora
NXP Semiconductors
Austin, USA
mohit.arora@me.com

ISBN 978-0-9972972-0-1   e-ISBN 978-0-9972972-1-8
Learning Bytes Publishing Austin

This book is dedicated to my daughters Janya and Prisha.

Preface

Ever since I got involved in chip design during my earlier career, designing IPs, I got more involved into SoC architecture, before taking a full time architect position focused on embedded systems. The role allowed me to visit customers world-wide, validate requirements, before starting to write detailed architectural specifications for the design team. During this course, I realized, though looks simple, embedded applications require some unique aspects that need specific attention to the chip architecture, much different than typical consumer applications that are mostly focused on features and processing capabilities.

This is my second book that is very natural extension of my first book titled "The Art of hardware architecture" that was focused on design techniques, while the current one extends that further to embedded systems architecture.

"Embedded System Design" could be perceived as broad term and may mean differently to different people/audience.

The book's aim is to highlight all the complex issues, tasks and techniques that must be mastered by a SoC Architect to define and architect SoC for an embedded application. Since "Embedded System design" is a broad subject, the first revision of the book does not cover everything but make an attempt to include essential elements and attributes that are important to design an embedded system. The subsequent version of the book will include extended topics to keep the book up-to date with any upcoming trends.

The book is intended for a wide audience. Though it may be used in an undergraduate or graduate course, book is mainly intended for those in semiconductor industries who are directly involved with chip design and requires deeper understand of the subject.

This book is distinguished from others by its primary focus on real problems rather than theoretical concepts with its emphasis on architectural techniques across various aspects of chip-design, especially focused on embedded systems.

The book covers aspects of embedded systems in a consistent way, starting with basic concepts in Chapter 1 that provides introduction to embedded systems and gradually increasing the depth to reach advanced concepts, such as power management and design consideration for maximum power efficiency and higher battery life.

Chapter 1 *"Introduction to Embedded systems"* help readers understand more clearly the key attributes of embedded systems and how they differentiate from general computer systems. This chapter includes some real-time examples of embedded system across variety of applications.

Chapter 2 *"Handling Interrupts"* covers all on how interrupts should be handled in an embedded system. Low Latency interrupt is the most important attribute for any embedded applications that needs special attention on how interrupts should be dealt with. Chapter describes various types of interrupts, Interrupt Service Routine (ISR), Interrupt vector table, Interrupt latency and methods to process interrupts for embedded application.

Chapter 3 *"Memory addressing"* starts with memory classification based on memory attributes, memory hierarchy and memory map. Chapter expands on how memory addressing system should be designed for an optimal performance. Chapter also covers how to handle endianness in design that that may include several third-party IPs with different Endianness and the way it can be handled in the design in an optimal way.

Chapter 4 focuses on all one need to know about embedded *"System Boot"*. The chapter starts with Window XP boot as an example to start with as that being very common consumer boot and expands the later sections to include boot process and options in an embedded application. The chapter includes challenges in embedded boot, Boot ROM and bootloaders for embedded application including popular open source universal bootloader (U-Boot).

Chapter 5 covers all about *"System Integrity"*. The chapter outlines the need for robust Watchdog and the guidelines that must be considered while designing a fault tolerant system monitor aka Watchdog.

Chapter 6 covers several hardware as well as software *"Debouncing Techniques"* to eliminate unwanted noise or glitch in the circuit caused by an external input (usually some kind of switch).

Chapter 7 covers deep details on *"Power Management"* that outlines power supply design models and design considerations to select the right regulation system for target application. The chapter also covers some of the real life power management examples for some of the popular embedded applications.

Theoretical part has been intentionally kept to the minimum that is essentially required to understand the subject. The guidelines explained across various chapters are independent of any CAD tool or silicon process and are applicable to any SoC architecture targeted for embedded systems.

Every possible effort was made to make the book self-contained. Any feedback/comments are welcome on this aspect or any other related aspects. Comments can be sent to me at the following mail: mohit.arora@me.com.

MOHIT ARORA, MAY 2016

Acknowledgements

The original idea behind *"Embedded System Design"* was to link my years of experience as a system architect with the practical experiences architecting SoC and meeting customers. However, achieving the final shape of this book would not have been possible without many contributions.

My sweet wife *Pooja* was so patient with my late nights, and I want to thank her for her faithful support & encouragement in writing this book. Most of the work occurred on weekends, nights, while on vacation, and other times inconvenient to my family. I like to thank my parents for allowing me to follow my ambitions throughout my childhood.

I am thankful to *Prashant Bhargava* from NXP Semiconductors for his careful reading of drafts of this book. He also helped in formatting apart from content reviews.

I am grateful to *Rob Cosaro* from NXP Semiconductors for his constructive suggestions for improvement based on his years of experience in embedded systems.

Special thanks to *Kumar Abhishek* and *Rakesh Pandey* from NXP Semiconductors for their early help and feedback on some of the sections of the book.

MOHIT ARORA, MAY 2016

Contents

1. Introduction to Embedded Systems

1.1 Introduction

There are millions of computing systems built every year destined for desktop computers (Personal Computers, or PC's), workstations, mainframes and servers. Interestingly there are rather billions of computing systems that are built every year for a very different purpose: they are embedded within larger devices, repeatedly carrying out a particular function, often going completely unrecognized by the device's user.

This Chapter is intended to help the readers understand about what makes system an embedded system, how it differs from general computer systems and other key components of an embedded systems.

1.2 Embedded Systems Overview

An embedded system is combination of computer hardware and software that is specifically designed for a particular function. However one will find the definition of embedded system difficult to generalize and constantly evolves with advances in technology. Below are some of the popular definitions:-

"Loosely defined, it is any device that includes a programmable computer but is not itself intended to be a general purpose computer" by Wayne Wolf [1]

"An embedded computer system includes a microcomputer with mechanical, chemical and electrical devices attached to it, programmed for a specific dedicated purpose, and packaged as a complete system" by Jonathan W. Valvano [2]

"Embedded Systems are the electronic systems that contain a microprocessor or a microcontroller, but we do not think of them as computers— the computer is hidden or embedded in the system." by Todd D. Morton [3]

One may not realize but will find embedded devices into all sort of everyday items. In fact one may find easily find more than dozen embedded devices in a home hidden or embedded inside things like washing machines, electronic shavers, Digital TV, digital cameras, air-conditioning etc. The key characteristic, however, is that an embedded system is designed to handle a particular task. Most embedded devices are primary designed for a particular function; however one may find several embedded devices, such as a Smartphone, Digital TVs etc. that may perform variety of functions.

Table 1-1 lists some of the *"Embedded Device"* examples across various markets.

Market	Embedded Device Example
Home	Washing Machine
	Refrigerator
	Microwave Oven
	Thermostat/Central heating controller
	Electronic Shaver
Automotive	Clusters
	Ignition control
	Braking System
	Engine Control
Office and Commerce	Printer
	Photocopier
	Coffee Machine
Medical	Infusion pumps
	Blood Pressure Monitor
	Dialysis machine
Industrial	Robotics
	Industrial Motors
	Elevator Control
	Energy Meter and Smart Grid
Consumer Electronics	Digital Television
	Cellphone/PDA/Pagers
	Set-Top Box
	Digital Watch
	Toys/games
Networking	Routers
	Gateways
	Hubs

Table 1-1 : Embedded Device Examples across various markets

For a typical embedded device, a user can make choices concerning the functionality but cannot change the system functionality by adding or replacing software. For example, a programmable digital thermostat has an embedded system that has a dedicated function of monitoring and controlling the surrounding temperature. User may have choices for setting the desired low and high temperatures but cannot just change its functionality to function something different than a temperature controller. The software for an embedded system is often referred to as firmware, and often contained in the system's non-volatile memory.

In most cases, an embedded system is used to replace an application-specific electronics in the consumer products. By doing so, most of the system's functionality is encapsulated in the firmware that runs the system, and it is possible to change and upgrade the system by changing the firmware, while keeping the hardware same.

Unless told, most of the users would be completely unaware that what they are using is controlled by one or more embedded device. Most people do recognize computers by their screen, keyboard, disc drives and so on. These embedded devices or computers have none of these characteristics. In the next section, we will discuss more details on embedded device and the main characteristics that differentiate them from general computers.

1.3 General versus Embedded System Design

Let's consider a computer. A computer is a system that has the following or more components:-

- A Microprocessor
- A large primary memory that includes RAM, ROM and cache.
- A large secondary memory like hard disk drive, optical drive or solid state drive.
- I/O unit such as display, keyboard, mouse and others.
- Operating System (OS)
- General purpose user interfaces and application software.

In comparison, an embedded system at minimum would include following components

- Embeds hardware that includes the core and necessary I/O for a specific function.
- Embeds main application software into embedded Flash.
- Embeds a real time operating system (RTOS) which supervises the application software tasks running on the hardware.

Following includes more specific characteristics exhibited by an embedded system:-

1. *Limited hardware and software functionality*: Embedded systems are usually limited in hardware and software functionality as compared to a personal computer (PC). Hardware limitation includes limited performance, reduced power consumption, memory as well as hardware functionality. In software, this includes limited operating system (OS) or even no OS and scale-down applications.

2. *Custom designed for a dedicated function:* As mentioned before, most embedded devices are primary designed for one specific function, while there may still be many hybrid embedded devices designed to be able to handle variety of primary functions. In comparison, general purpose system could be used to run any program of your choice.

3. *High quality and reliability:* This may be application specific, but some embedded devices are highly reliable and can work for long operation hours without failure. For example if a medical device fails during a surgery or car engine controller crashes in the middle of the road or if car airbags fail to work during a crash can lead to serious problems. In comparison personal computer system may often crash and may cause inconvenience but not usually a life threatening situation.

4. *Low Latency and real time operation*: Due to nature of the application, some embedded systems are predominantly interrupt controlled where task performed by the system are triggered by different kind of internal counter or events, thus providing low latency operation. For example medical robot performing a surgical procedure , say a fine incision on a vital organ, needs fast response(i.e low latency) to a command to be able to take an action in case of a failure to avoid any further damage. Often these embedded system use simple OS or real time operating system (RTOS) to provide determinism, that a particular operation would be executed in certain defined timeframe.

Embedded systems are typically used over long periods of time, will not (or cannot) be programmed or maintained by its end-users, and often face significantly different design constraints such as limited memory, low cost, strict performance guarantees, fail-safe operation, low power, reliability and guaranteed real-time behavior.

These embedded systems often use simple executives (OS kernels) or real-time operating systems with typically small footprints, support for real-time scheduling and no hard drives. Many embedded systems also interact with their physical environment using a variety of sensors and/or actuators.

1.4 Embedded Systems Examples

1.4.1 Air Conditioning System

The main job of an air conditioner is to cool the indoor air. Air conditioners monitor and regulate the air temperature via a thermostat. Air conditioners function also acts as dehumidifiers. Because temperature is a key component of relative humidity, reducing the temperature of a volume of humid air causes it to release a portion of its moisture. That's why there are drains and moisture-collecting pans near or attached to air conditioners, and the reason for why air conditioners discharge water when they operate on humid days.

If you open a window air conditioner unit, you will find that it contain following main components:-

- *Evaporator* – Receives the liquid refrigerant
- *Condenser* – Facilitates heat transfer
- *Compressor* – A pump that pressurizes refrigerant
- *Expansion Value* – Regulates refrigerant flow into evaporator
- *Fans* – Usually two
- *Hot Coil* – On the outside
- *Cold Coil* – On the inside

The cold side of an air conditioner contains the evaporator and a fan that blows air over the chilled coils and into the room. The hot side contains the compressor, condenser and another fan to vent hot air coming off the compressed refrigerant to the outdoors. In between the two sets of coils, there's an expansion valve. It regulates the amount of compressed liquid refrigerant moving into the evaporator. Once in the evaporator, the refrigerant experiences a pressure drop, expands and changes back into a gas. The compressor is actually a large electric pump that pressurizes the refrigerant gas as part of the process of turning it back into a liquid. There are many additional and optional components like sensors, timers and valves, but the evaporator, compressor, condenser and expansion valve are the main components of an air conditioner.

This forms the basic setup for a conventional air-conditioner. Window air conditioners have all these components mounted into a relatively small metal box that installs into a window opening. The hot air vents from the back of the unit, while the condenser coils and a fan cool and re-circulate indoor air. A split-system air conditioner splits the hot side from the cold side of the system with the hot side usually kept outside the building/Room.

Older Air-conditioners were mechanical with limited electronics and based on discrete solution with no value added features. All new generation Air-conditioners include microcontroller that adds lot of smart features. An example is shown in Figure 1-1.

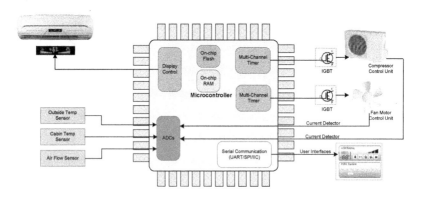

Figure 1-1: Embedded System Example: Air conditioner

On-chip analog to digital converters (ADCs) will keep on monitoring the temperature via various temperature sensors. If at all the room temperature changes due to variation in external temperature, controller will take a counter acting signal to the compressor and temperature will be brought to required range. PWM could be used to control the compressor motor frequency and fan speed. ADCs could monitor the varying compressor motor frequency and signal the on-chip multi-channel Timers (via CPU) to create most efficient PWM waveforms for the motor speed, resulting in better efficiency and low power consumption.

Electronically controlled motor drives (i.e IGBT) could be either discrete (as shown in the figure) or integrated and come in varying switching frequency to increase efficiency. Other components included display controller to directly drive segmented display or multiple serial communication interfaces like UART, IIC, and SPIs for user-interface like buttons, knobs for HVAC control. This could even include touch-sensing or communication modules like Zigbee to be able to communicate with Home Area Network and provide energy information.

1.4.2 Automotive Airbag Control

Stopping an object's momentum requires force acting over a period of time. When a car crashes, the force required to stop an object is very high because the car's momentum has changed instantly while the passengers' has not. The goal of any supplemental restraint system is to help stop the passenger while doing as little damage to him or her as possible.

What an airbag does is to slow the passenger's speed to zero with little or no damage; however the constraints that it has to work within are huge. The goal of an airbag is to slow the passenger's forward motion as evenly as possible in a fraction of a second. For the front driver airbag, a bag made of thin, nylon fabric, is folder into the steering wheel (as shown in the Figure 1-2). A sensor in the device (part of microcontroller explained later in this section) indicates a bag to inflate during a collision. Inflation is a result of chemical reaction to produce nitrogen gas that inflates the airbag.

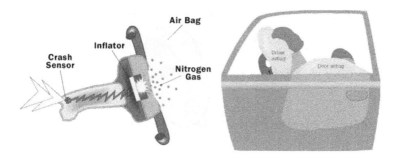

Figure 1-2: Automotive Airbag Control

Whole process happens in few milliseconds, thus require a microcontroller to control the whole operation.

Figure 1-3 shows microcontroller that is the heart for airbag control unit to manage the whole operation. A microcontroller monitors a number of sensors such as G-sensors, front sensors and Rollover sensors. When a predefined threshold is exceeded, it sends a signal to trigger the ignition of the airbags via special squib driver circuits.

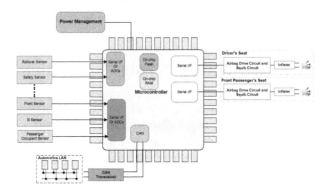

Figure 1-3: Microcontroller for Airbag control

Usually microcontroller based on 16-bit or 32-bit microcontroller would provide better performance and lower latency to crash event. Some high-end cars may even go further and add additional core in a microcontroller to provide fail safe operation.

CAN connectivity allows to communicate with other modules to provide additional information. On-chip ADC (would be 12-bit or more for higher accuracy) would allow to interface to various sensors as shown.

As an additional safety factor, highly-efficient switched-mode power supply components allow the system to keep operating for several hundred milliseconds if the battery connection is lost during an accident.

1.4.3 Blood Pressure Monitoring Machine

There are two numbers in a blood pressure reading: systolic and diastolic. Systolic arterial pressure is the higher blood pressure reached by the arteries during systole (ventricular contraction), and diastolic arterial pressure is the lowest blood pressure reached during diastole (ventricular relaxation). In a healthy young adult at rest, systolic arterial pressure is around 120 mmHg and diastolic arterial pressure is around 80 mmHg.

Blood flow is the blood volume that flows through any tissue in a determined period of time (typically represented as ml/min) in order to bring tissue oxygen and nutrients transported in blood. Blood flow is directly affected by the blood pressure as blood flows from the area with more pressure to the area with less pressure. Greater the pressure difference, higher is the blood flow. Blood is pumped from the left ventricle of the heart out to the aorta where it reaches its higher pressure levels. Blood pressure falls as blood moves away from the left ventricle until it reaches 0 mm Hg, when it returns to the heart's right atrium.

Blood pressure monitor operation is based on the oscillometric method. This method takes advantage of the pressure pulsations taken during measurements. An occluding cuff is placed on the left arm and is connected to an air pump and a pressure sensor. Cuff is inflated until a pressure greater than the typical systolic value is reached, then the cuff is slowly deflated. As the cuff deflates, when systolic pressure value approaches, pulsations start to appear. These pulsations represent the pressure changes due to heart ventricle contraction and can be used to calculate the heartbeat rate. Pulsations grow in amplitude until mean arterial pressure (MAP) is reached, then decrease until they disappear.

Oscillometric method determines the MAP by taking the cuff pressure when the pulse with the largest amplitude appears. Systolic and diastolic values are calculated using algorithms that vary among different medical equipment developers.

Figure 1-4 shows blood pressure monitor based on a microcontroller.

The arm cuff is inflated using an external air pump controlled with an MCU GPIO pin, and deflated by activating an escape valve with another GPIO pin.

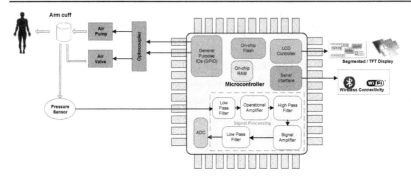

Figure 1-4: Microcontroller for Blood Pressure Monitor

One way to activate air pump is to provide current through USB however current through the USB port may not be enough to activate the air pump and the valve, so another option would be to activate the external components using an external power source (like dual AA 1.5V batteries) which provides sufficient current. An optocoupler (as shown) is needed for coupling MCU control signals with the components to activate. Output from the optocoupler is connected to a MOSFET working as a switch, so the air pump and valve mechanisms can be activated successfully.

The functionality of the oscillometric method is based on the measurement of the pressure variations in the arm cuff. Pressure in the cuff is measured by using the Pressure Sensor which may be integrated on-chip or off-chip. Signal processing is usually done as part of microcontroller. Typical components may include a low pass filter (LPF) to remove high frequency noise, a buffer circuit consisting of single Op-Amp in buffer mode to couple the signal to the sensor. The output from the buffer circuit is where the arterial pressure measurements are taken. Signal is then filtered with a high pass filter (HPF) to remove high-frequency noise and get a cleaner signal for amplification. Resulting signal is then amplified using non-inverting amplifier with another low pass filter to remove high frequency noise. However signal processing can vary with vendors.

Also shown LCD controller to support variety of segmented or TFT display and number of connectivity options to interface external communication modules directly with micro-controller. Internal Microcontroller Flash will retain custom measurement algorithms that would again be specific to Original Equipment Manufacturer (OEM).

1.4.4 Smart Electricity Meter

An energy meter is a device that measures the amount of electrical energy supplied to a residential or commercial building. The most common unit of measurement made by a meter is the kilowatt hour, which is equal to the amount of energy used by a load of one kilowatt in one hour.

Figure 1-5 shows a system block diagram for a three phase energy meter. As shown the energy meter hardware includes a power supply, an analog front end, a microcontroller section, and an interface section. The analog front end is the part that interfaces to the high voltage lines. It converts high voltages and high currents to voltages sufficiently small to be measured directly by the ADC (Analog to Digital Converter) of the microcontroller.

Voltage measurement is done with a shunt resister (shown as "*Load*"), while the current measurements require more precise measurement and thus are done by Current Transformer (CT) on all phases along with current measurement on neutral. Meter manufacturers often integrate gain amplifiers in order to amplify voltage as well as current measurements in the range supported by the ADC. The amount of amplification required depends on the ADC resolution as well as the Class accuracy (0.1, 0.2. 1.0 etc.) required for a three phase meter.

A typical energy meter also requires a Real Time Clock (RTC) for tariff information. The RTC required for a metering application needs to be very accurate (< 5ppm) for Time of Day (TOD), which involves dividing the day, month and year into tariff slots. Higher rates are applied at peak load periods and lower tariff rates at off-peak load periods.

The heart of the meter is the firmware, which calculates Active, reactive energy based on voltage and current measurement. The firmware also includes tamper detection algorithms, data logging and protocols like DLMS and Power Line Modem communication protocol for Automatic Meter Reading (AMR).

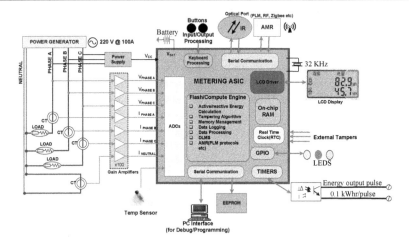

Figure 1-5: System Block Diagram for three phase Energy Meter

The energy meter also needs to be calibrated before it can be used and that is done in a digital domain for an electronic meter. Digital calibration is fast, efficient and can be automated, removing the time-consuming manual trimming required in traditional, electromechanical meters. Calibration coefficients are safely stored in an EEPROM that can be either internal or external.

An energy pulse output (EP) is an indication of active power, as registered by the meter; the frequency of the pulse is directly proportional to active power.

1.4.5 Portable Music Player

Portability is a large factor in the popularity of the music or more commonly called as "MP3" player, considering the ease of transportation in comparison to a CD player and CD storage case in the old days. MP3, or MPEG Audio Layer III, is one method for compressing audio files. MPEG is the acronym for Moving Picture Experts Group, a group that has developed compression systems for video data, including that for DVD movies, HDTV broadcasts and digital satellite systems. Using the MP3 compression system reduces the number of bytes in a song, while retaining sound that is near CD-quality, however requires the player to be able to decompress the audio before playing it.

A Portable music player is a convergence of many technologies. Unlike earlier forms of music players that required moving parts to read encoded data on a tape or CD, MP3 players use solid-state memory. An MP3 player is no more than a data-storage device with an embedded software application that allows users to transfer MP3 files to the player and play them. The advantage to solid-state memory is that there are no moving parts, which means better reliability.

The microprocessor is the brains of the player. It monitors user input through the playback controls, displays information about the current song on the LCD panel and sends directions to the DSP engine (could be part of the Chip as shown in the Figure 1-6 or separate chip) that tells it exactly how to process the audio.

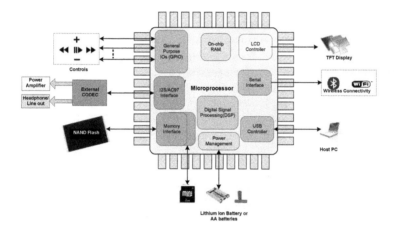

Figure 1-6: Microprocessor based Portable music player

In addition to storing music, the music or MP3 player must play music and allow the user to hear the songs played. To do this, the player pulls the song from its memory, decompresses the MP3 encoding through DSP, via an algorithm or formula. Runs the decompressed bytes through a CODEC that includes a digital-to-analog converter to convert the data into sound waves and amplifies the analog signal, allowing the song to be heard.

All of the portable MP3 players are battery-powered. Most branded would use a rechargeable internal lithium battery that would last for number of hours on a single charge. Charging Lithium Ion battery via USB port is now a common supported feature of most portable customer grade devices including media player.

1.5 Components of Embedded Systems

An Embedded System includes three main components:-

- Hardware
- Application Software
- Real time Operating System (RTOS)

Embedded Hardware:

Hardware for an embedded system would typically include the following:-

Power Management: This includes the power supply and additional control to be able to support variety of power modes, some of them including power gating modes to offer number of operating modes thus optimizing power consumption for hand-held devices. System may even choose to retain some of the peripherals like Real Time Clock (RTC) if main supply is lost by running it on batteries.

Embedded Processor: This is the heart of any microcontroller based embedded system. These are optimized for general purpose use providing lower size and just the right functionality for an embedded product as compared to microprocessors used in desktop PCs that have all the bells and whistles. Most of this class of processor would include some basic DSP functionality including hardware multiplier and divider for some of the applications that require them.

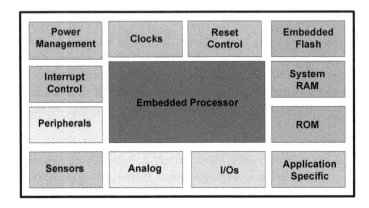

Figure 1-7: Hardware view for an embedded Microcontroller

Embedded Memory: The memory unit in an embedded system should have low access time and high density. Some of the embedded microcontrollers include ROM as primary bootloader that is pre-programmed by the vendor. The contents of ROM are non-volatile (power failure does not erase the contents). All embedded microcontroller include some sort of system memory or RAM (volatile) to store transient input or output data. Embedded systems generally do not possess secondary storage devices such as magnetic disks. As programs of embedded systems are small there is no need for virtual storage.

A microcontroller will always include an embedded Flash, for the program memory. This is especially true for system that does not include complete OS and can fit in small Flash embedded in the microcontroller.

Peripherals and I/Os: Peripherals are the input and output devices connected to the serial and parallel ports of the embedded system. Serial ports transfer one bit at a time between the peripheral and the microcontroller or microprocessor. Parallel ports transfer an entire word consisting of many bits simultaneously between the peripheral and the microcontroller. A microcontroller generally communicates with the peripherals using a programmable interface device. Programmable interface devices provide flexibility since they can be programmed to perform I/O on different peripherals. The microcontroller monitors the inputs from peripherals and performs actions when certain events occur. For instance, when sensors indicate that the level of water in the wash tub of a washing machine is above the preset level, the microprocessor starts the wash cycle.

Timers and Watchdog: To be able to time events, a microcontroller would typically include various timers, including the one fully operational in low power mode was quicker recovery and exit from low power modes. Another special timer *"watchdog timer"* is also an essential part of any embedded system that is used to detect and recover from code runaway or other malfunctions.

Sensors and Analog: Microcontroller for an embedded device would often include lot of sensors like temperature sensor and analog modules like Analog to Digital converter (ADC), Digital to Analog converter, Operational Amplifiers for signal conditioning and sensing. One good example would be for battery voltage to be monitored constantly by ADC and generate an interrupt to indicate application software before getting drained completely.

Interrupt Controller: Due to real time nature for some of the embedded applications, an embedded system would often require low latency and fast response to an interrupt event. This could be one of the important considerations for selecting a microcontroller for microprocessor for an embedded device. Apart from interrupt controller, chip architecture and way caches and RAMs are organized plays a big role to achieve low latency response.

Clocking and Reset: A microcontroller for embedded system would include number of clock options including external crystal and internal oscillators, providing choice of low power and quick start up. Typically Power-on-Reset (POR) circuitry would also be included as a part of microcontroller in comparison to general system.

Application Specific: Some of the embedded applications would also include application specific logic as part of microcontroller or microprocessor.

Note: *Microprocessor and Microcontroller are used interchangeably in this section, however later Section 1.6 will cover details on how microcontroller differentiates with Microprocessor.*

Note: *Features described in this section for embedded system hardware just covers general trends and options, however does not mean all embedded system hardware would include all the options described above.*

Application Software and RTOS:

Due to the absence of secondary storage devices in an embedded system, program code resides in embedded Flash or ROM. During execution of the program, storage space for variables is allocated in the RAM. The programs should execute continuously and should be capable of handling all possible exceptional conditions. Hence the programs generally do not call the function exit.

Real-time embedded systems possess an RTOS (real-time operating system). The RTOS consists of a scheduler that manages the execution of multiple tasks in the embedded systems. Unlike operating systems for the desktop computers where scheduling deadlines are not critical, an RTOS should schedule tasks and interrupt service routines such that they are completed within their deadlines. So in summary RTOS sets the rules during execution of application processes to enable finishing of a process within the assigned time interval and with assigned priority.

The RTOS provides features that simplify the programmer's job. For example, an RTOS provides semaphores that can be used by the programmer to prevent multiple tasks from simultaneously writing into shared memory.

With the recent developments in VLSI, the processor, memory, peripherals and the interfaces to the outside world (as explained earlier in this section) are integrated into a single chip resulting in a microcontroller.

1.6 Microprocessor versus Microcontroller

A *microprocessor* is a general-purpose digital computer central processing unit. To make a complete microcomputer, number of additional components like additional memory (ROM and RAM), Interfaces and I/O ports are required as shown in the Figure 1-8.

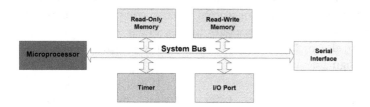

Figure 1-8: Microprocessor based System

As shown in the figure, all support devices like Read-only Memory, Read-Write Memory, Serial Interface, Timers and I/O Port are all external and interfaced to Microprocessor via system bus. The system bus is composed of address bus, data bus and control bus. The prime use of a microprocessor is to read data, perform extensive calculations on that data, and store the results in a mass storage device or display the results. Some of the popular microprocessor examples include 8085, 8086, Z80, 6800, Pentium, Intel i3, Intel i5, Intel i7 processors.

The design of the microcontroller is driven by the desire to make it as expandable and flexible as possible. A Microcontroller is a functional computer system-on-a-chip. It contains a processor, memory, and programmable input/output peripherals. Microcontrollers include an integrated processor, memory (a small amount of RAM, program memory, or both) and peripherals capable of input and output. In summary, a microcontroller is nothing but a microprocessor system with all support devices integrated inside a single chip (see Figure 1-9).

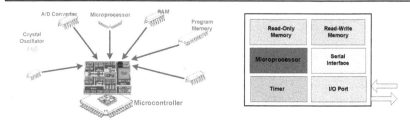

Figure 1-9: Microcontroller based system

Even though the microprocessor is considered to be a powerful computer machine, the weak point is that it is not adjusted to communication to peripheral environment. Simply, in order to communicate with peripheral environment, the microprocessor must use specialized circuits added as external chips (see Figure 1-9). It means in short that microprocessors are the pure heart of the computers. That is how it was when they appeared and the same is now. On the other hand, the microcontroller is designed to be all of that in one. No other specialized external components are needed for its application because all necessary circuits which otherwise belong to peripherals are already built into it. It in any case saves the time and space needed to design a device.

In addition, Microcontrollers offer software protection whereas Microprocessor based system fails to offer a protection system. This is made possible in microcontrollers by locking the on-chip program memory which makes it difficult to read using an external circuit.

Some of the popular microcontroller examples include 68HC05/08, PIC 16F8X, 8051, 68HC11xx, Intel 80960A, ARM 7, ARM Cortex M, Power PC MPC 604.

Generally in the embedded world, the term *"MPU"* is used for *"Micro processing unit"* or *"Microprocessor"* that does not include Flash(Flash being external to MCU) in the System-on-chip. Likewise the term *"MCU"* is used for *"Microcontroller"* that includes on-chip Flash in the system-on-chip.

1.7 Program and Data Memory

Any embedded system will include a memory unit to store and retrieve digital information. This includes program memory and data memory that form one of the key elements of a microcontroller. Program Memory is used for permanent saving program being executed, while Data Memory is used for temporarily storing and keeping intermediate results and variables.

Program Memory:

Program Memory is used to execute the permanent saving program or more popularly called *"program code"*, and is divided into two sections, Boot Program and the Application Program.

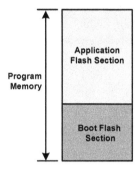

Figure 1-10: Program Memory

Some of the microcontrollers keep the size of the section configurable. These two sections can have different level of protection attributes. Depending on the settings made in compiler, program memory may also be used to store constant variables.

Some Microcontrollers would keep the Boot portion in a physically separate read only memory, often a ROM, while keeping rest of the program memory in on-chip Flash.

Data Memory:

Data memory is the volatile memory that is used to store the variables during the program execution and is deleted once the power to the microcontroller is lost. Data Memory would often include the following:-

- General purpose registers
- I/O Memory
- Extended I/O Memory (MCU dependent)
- Internal RAM

Data memory includes several general purpose registers proving shortest (fastest) access time, often allowing single cycle Arithmetic Logic Unit (ALU) operations.

I/O Memory space contains addresses for CPU peripheral function, such as Control registers, SPI, and other I/O functions.

Due to the complexity, some microcontrollers with more peripherals include Extended I/O memory, which occupies part of the internal SRAM. Extended I/O memory is MCU dependent.

Storing data in I/O and Extended I/O memory is usually handled by the compiler only. Users can not use this memory space for storing their data. Internal SRAM (Data Memory) is used for temporarily storing and keeping intermediate results and variables.

So both program memory and data memory have a different role in building a program. Program Memory must be a non-volatile memory (often on-chip or off-chip Flash), which store the information even after the power is turn off. In contrast, Data Memory does not save the information because it needs power in order to maintain the information stored in the chip.

The Program memory in a personal computer is implemented exactly this way. It has a fixed part of program memory that contains the *basic input/output system* (BIOS). These programs are permanently held in a read-only memory device mounted on the main processor board. Programs held this way in ROM are called *firmware* because of their permanent nature. The typically size of a BIOS ROM used in a PC today is 2 megabits (MB), which equal 256Kbytes. The much larger part of the program storage memory in a PC is built with dynamic random access read/write memory devices (DRAMs). They may be either mounted on the main processor board or on an add-in memory module or board. Use of DRAMs allows this part of the program storage memory to be either read from or written into. Its purpose is again to store programs that are to be executed, but in this case they are loaded into memory only when needed. Programs are normally read in from the secondary storage device (HDD or Flash), stored in the program storage part of memory, and then run. When the program is terminated, the part of the program memory where it resides is given back to the operating system for reuse. Moreover, if power is turned off, the contents of the RAM based part of the program storage memory are lost. Due to the temporary nature of these programs, they are referred to as software.

In the PC world, due to small size of the BIOS, major part of the primary storage is DRAM to be used for program storage. In comparison, in an embedded system, such as an electronic game or coffee machine, the complete program storage memory is implemented with either ROM or Flash devices.

As explained before, information that frequently changes is stored in the data storage part of the memory subsystem. For instance, the data to be processed by the microcomputer or microcontroller is held in the data storage part of the primary storage memory. When a program is run, the values of the data can change repeatedly. For this reason, data storage memory must be implemented with RAM. In a PC, the data does not automatically reside in the data storage part of memory. Just like software, it is read into memory from a secondary storage device, such as the hard disk. Any part of the PCs DRAM can be then assigned for data storage. This is all managed by the operating system software. When a program is run, data are modified while in DRAM and writing them to the disk saves the new values. Data does not have to be numeric in form; they can also be alphanumeric characters, codes, and graphical patterns. For instance, when running a word processor application, the data are alphanumeric and graphical information.

1.8 Microcontroller Selection Criteria

Selecting the proper microcontroller unit (MCU) for an application is one of the critical decisions which control the success or failure of a project. There are numerous criteria to consider when choosing an MCU and this section will enumerate most of them, however the main goal is to select the least expensive MCU that minimizes the overall cost of the system while still fulfilling the system specification.

NOTE: *Engineers must have their own criteria in order to make the right selection. This section discusses the general considerations and some guidelines to keep in mind when selecting a microcontroller, serving as a basis for setting your own criteria.*

To start the selection process, the designer must first ask, "*What does the MCU need to do in my system?*" The answer to this one simple question dictates the required MCU features for the system and, thus, is the controlling agency in the selection process.

The second step is to conduct a search for MCUs which meet all of the system requirements. This usually involves searching the literature - primarily data books, data sheets, and technical trade journals but also includes peer consultations. If the fit is good enough, a single-chip MCU solution has been found; otherwise, a second search must be conducted to find an MCU which best fits the requirements with a minimum of extra circuitry, including considerations of cost and board space. Obviously, a single-chip solution is preferred for cost as well as reliability reasons. Of course, if there is a company policy dictating which MCU manufacturer to use, this will narrow the search considerably. The last step has several parts, all of which attempt to reduce the list of acceptable MCUs to a single choice. These parts include pricing, availability, development tools, manufacturer support, stability, and sole sourcing. The whole process may need to be iterated several times to arrive at the optimum decision.

General MCU Attributes:

MCUs generally can be classified into 8-bit, 16-bit, and 32-bit groups based upon the size of their arithmetic and index register(s), although some designers argue that bus access size determines the 8-, 16-, 32-bit architecture.

- Is a lower-cost 8-bit MCU able to handle the requirements of the system, or is a higher-cost 16-bit or 32-bit MCU required?
- Can 8-bit software simulation of features found on the 16-bit or 32-bit MCUs permit using the lower-cost 8-bit MCU by sacrificing some code size and speed? For example, can an 8-bit MCU be used with software macros to implement 16-bit accumulator and indexing operations? The choice of implementation language (high-level) versus assembler) can greatly affect system throughput, which can then dictate the choice of 8-, 16-, and 32-bit architectures, but system cost restraints may override this [4].

Clock speed, or more accurately bus speed, determines how much processing can be accomplished in a given amount of time by the MCU. Some MCUs have a narrow clock speed range, whereas others can operate down to zero. Sometimes a specific clock frequency is chosen to generate another clock required in the system, for example, for serial baud rates. In general, computational power, power consumption, and system cost increase with higher clock frequencies. System costs increase with frequency because not only does the MCU cost more, but so do all the support chips required, such as RAMs, ROMs, PLDs (programmable logic device), and bus drivers.

Memory Requirements:

The size of memory may be an important consideration. Some microcontrollers have just few instruction and limited RAM for example 16 bytes of RAM. Some microcontroller family have relatively small memory limits imposed by their architecture, some algorithms require substantial RAM to be implemented in a straightforward manner, and it may be worthwhile looking for a microcontrollers with a lot of RAM (or external RAM expansion capabilities) if that is a critical need.

Peripherals and on-chip resources:

By definition, all MCUs have on-chip resources to achieve a higher level of integration and reliability at a lower cost. An on-chip resource is a block of circuitry built into the MCU which performs some useful function under control of the MCU. Built-in resources increase reliability because they do not require any external circuitry to be working for the resource to function. They are pre-tested by the manufacturer and conserve board space by integrating the circuitry into the MCU. This category also includes on-chip memory and memory expansion capability that has been already covered in *"Memory Requirements"* section.

Most common peripherals could include timers, both real-time clocks and periodic interrupt timers. Be sure to consider the range and resolution of the timer as well as any sub functions, such as timer compare and/or input capture lines. I/O includes serial communication ports, parallel ports (I/O lines), analog-to-digital (A/D) converters, digital-to-analog (D/A) converters, liquid crystal display drivers (LCD). Certainly if one wants microcontroller to have built in Ethernet, CAN, USB, or even multiple serial ports, many common choices are going to be eliminated. It's also convenient if output pins can supply reasonable amounts of current for driving LEDs or transistors directly; some chips have 5mA or less drive capability.

Some peripherals can be handy to have: UARTs, SPI or I2C controllers, PWM controllers, and EEPROM data memory are good examples, even though similar functionality can frequently be implemented in software or external parts. The less common built-in resources are internal/external bus capability, computer operating properly watchdog system, clock detection and selectable memory configurations.

On most MCUs with on-chip resources, a configuration register block is included to control these resources. Sometimes the configuration register block itself can be set up to appear at a different location in the memory map. Sometimes a user and/or factor test register is present, which indicates concern for quality by the manufacturer.

With configuration registers also comes the possibility of errant code altering the desired configuration, so check for "*lock-out*" mechanisms. For example, before a register can be changed, a bit in another register must first be altered in a certain sequence. Although configuration registers can at first be very confusing and intimidating because of their complexity, they are extremely valuable because of the flexibility they offer at a low cost so that a single MCU can serve many applications.

Physical Packaging:

Some OEMs just prefer QFP package than BGA due to ease in mounting, soldering and fabrication cost. However for applications that need small form factor due to physical geometry of the product, BGA may be a better solution. Similarly for security related applications, one would want to go with BGA package even though cost is high due to the fact that pins in the BGA package are not easy to probe as compared to QFP/DIP package, thus providing another later of security. It is often a combination of application needs and cost that drives the choice of package.

Microcontroller Architecture:

The "*architecture*" of a microcontroller refers to the philosophy of the internal implementation. It includes details like how many "*registers*" there are, and how "*general purpose*" those registers are, whether code can execute out of data memory, whether the peripherals are treated like memory, registers, or yet something else, whether there is a stack and how it works, and so on.

In a *"Harvard architecture"*, the instruction memory and the data memory are separate, controlled by different buses, and sometimes have different sizes. For microcontrollers, the instructions are usually stored in *"read only"* memory, and data is in RAM or registers.

In a *"Von Neuman Architecture"*, data and instructions share memory space, so you could do things like dynamic compilation to generate instructions in RAM and then execute them.

Microcontrollers are characterized by having small amounts of program (flash memory) and data (SRAM) memory, with no cache, and take advantage of the Harvard architecture to speed processing by concurrent instruction and data access. The separate storage means the program and data memories can have different bit widths, for example using 16-bit wide instructions and 8-bit wide data. They also mean that instruction pre-fetch can be performed in parallel with other activities. Examples include, the AVR by Atmel Corp, the PIC by Microchip Technology, Inc. and the ARM Cortex-M3 processor (not all ARM chips have Harvard architecture).

The principal advantage of the pure Harvard architecture—simultaneous access to more than one memory system—has been reduced by modified Harvard processors using modern CPU cache systems [5]. Relatively pure Harvard architecture machines are used mostly in applications where tradeoffs, such as the cost and power savings from omitting caches, outweigh the programming penalties from having distinct code and data address spaces.

MCU Instruction Set:

The instruction set and registers of each MCU should be considered carefully, as they play critical roles in the capability of the system. Some of the related questions to ask would be

- Are there any specialty instructions available which could be used in your system, such as multiply, divide, and table lookup/interpolate?
- Are there any bit manipulation instructions (bit set, bit clear, bit test, bit change, branch on bit set, branch on bit clear) to allow easier implementation of controller applications?
- How about big field instructions?

A Microcontroller may support lot of fancy instructions that seem to do a lot in one instruction however the real measure should be number of clocks it takes to accomplish the task at hand, not how many instructions were executed. A fair comparison is to code the same routine and compare the total number of clock cycles executed and bytes used.

MCU Interrupts:

Examining the interrupt structure is a necessity when constructing a real-time System. For instance one could look at:-

- How many interrupt lines or levels are there versus how many does your system require?
- Is there an interrupt level mask?
- Once an interrupt level is acknowledged, are there individual vectors to the interrupt handler routines or must each possible interrupt source be polled to determine the source of the interrupt?

In speed critical applications, such as controlling a printer, the interrupt response time, for example, the time from the start of the interrupt until the first instruction in the appropriate interrupt handler is executed, can be the selection criterion in determining the right MCU.

Hardware Tools:

Hardware tools (sort of programmer) are required to load the program into the microcontroller; however they vary widely in cost. It is pretty common for manufactures to offer some low cost development tools, however it may help further if manufactures support third party tools allowing more options for the development community.

Software Tools:

Most of the microcontrollers have some level of standard tools (at least an assembler) provided by the manufacturer. Most have "*Integrated Development Environments*" (IDE) that allow integrated use of an editor with the assembler, some compilers, and a simulator. Some have significant additional support from the open source movement.

Literature Support:

Literature covers a wide selection of printed material which can assist in the selection process. This includes items from the manufacturer, such as data sheets, data books, and application notes, as well as items available at the local book store and/or library. Book store and library items indicate not only the popularity of the manufacturers and MCUs under consideration, but they also offer unbiased opinions when written by non-manufacturer-related authors.

As a final step to help in the selection process, user should consider building a table to list each MCU under consideration on one axis and the important attributes on the other axis. Blanks should be filled in from the manufacturer's data sheets to obtain a fair side-by-side comparison. Some manufacturers have premade comparison sheets of their MCU product line which makes this task much easier, but as with all data sheets, be sure they are up-to-date with current production units.

NOTE: *There are other non-technical consideration like manufacturer support, company financials, and product roadmap for easy future upgrade and migration and other manufacturer attributes, however that is beyond the scope of this book.*

1.9 Embedded System Design Challenges

The embedded-system designer must of course construct an implementation that fulfills desired functionality, but a difficult challenge is to construct an implementation that simultaneously optimizes numerous design attributes.

Figure 1-11 shows some of the design parameters/attributes that control the success of an embedded system.

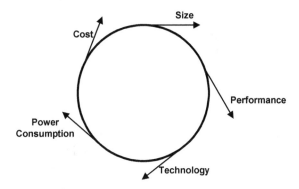

Figure 1-11: Parameters that Control embedded System Success

These design attributes typically compete with one another: improving one often leads to degradation in another. For example, if die size is reduced, thereby reducing the features, performance of embedded system may suffer. One may choose to move to lower technology node to reduce the die size and cost, however that may increase the leakage significant to have an adverse impact on power consumption.

Performance:-

Embedded system performance is not just about typical processor speed, what really matters is real-time performance, for example how quickly system reacts to specific event. An embedded system, often running a Real Time Operating System (RTOS) often guarantee a response within specific time window, thus offering determinism as compared to typical desktop computing where response is non-deterministic and not really critical.

Systems used for many mission critical applications must be real-time, such as for control of fly-by-wire aircraft, or anti-lock brakes on a vehicle, which must produce maximum deceleration but intermittently stop braking to prevent skidding [6]. Real-time processing fails if not completed within a specified deadline relative to an event; deadlines must always be met, regardless of system load.

Power Consumption:-

Low power consumption is a critical parameter for an embedded system. Compared to desktop PC or computer that is always powered, many embedded system are powered by battery. An embedded system has often a conflicting need for low power consumption and more performance.

Some applications may be continuously powered by battery like a water meter or Gas meter that measures the flow of water in a residential or commercial complex. Meter is required to work for several years without replacing the battery. So often these meters have ultra-low power mode (since they would be idle and kept in low power modes for majority of their life-cycle thus it is important to optimize them accordingly) that enable them to measure consumption with processor in sleep mode, only to enable them when counter overflows or data is to be send to remote network via communication media.

An embedded system never includes heat sink and must operate fan less unlike laptop or desktop PC. This increase the challenge to think beyond just active mode to optimize power consumption of an embedded system offering several low power modes.

Technology, size and design cost:-

Unlike in the desktop world where performance requirement drives the technology choice, there are number of factors that affect that decision in designing an embedded system. Since an embedded system needs to be highly reliable to be able to work in extreme conditions, some for long operational hours without failure, it is generally recommended selecting a stable technology node that is well tested under extreme conditions. Further it is reasonable to assume that a system-on-chip for an embedded product would include lot of analog blocks like ADC, DAC, Integrated Power management etc. that are tuned to specific technology and thus need to be re-designed every time a new technology node is adopted, adding significant risk and design cost. Further as indicated before, switching between different technology nodes can have significant impact on power consumption of the device and low power modes, thus affecting chip architecture.

Since switching between technology nodes adds huge NRE cost, volume have to be significantly high to be able to justify the same. In order to reduce per unit cost of embedded SoC, it is necessary to reduce the die size either by restricting feature set or by switching to lower technology node, which may be a natural transition once the technology is stable and transition cost is justified. So there is always a fine balance between Technology, die size and design cost when designing SoC for an embedded application.

Interoperability:-

Internet of Things (IoT) ecosystem have pushed several embedded devices to create the *"seamless"* programmability of the very devices or sensors that enables the full potential of a connected experience [7]. Since these embedded devices come from different manufactures, the lack of standard interfaces in the IoT space creates a big challenge for these devices to work together seamlessly.

Reliability:-

The amount of software (and technology) in products is increasing exponentially. However software is far from errorless. Studies of the density of errors in actual code show that 1000 lines of code typically contain 3 errors [8]. Incremental increase of the code size will increase the number of hidden errors in a system.

This may be application specific, but some embedded devices require high reliability and should be capable to work for long operation hours without failure. For example a medical device used in critical care cannot afford a crash which is common and often harmless in case of personal computers.

Security:-

Several stakeholders have significant different security interests. Following shows some examples categories with different interest and security requirement.

- Government and companies, which implement restrictive rules, which can be rather privacy intrusive.
- Consumers, who want to maintain privacy and at the same time usability of services.
- The content industry, who want to get fair payment for content creation and distribution. Their solution is again very restrictive, even violating the right of private copies, and characterized by a paranoia attitude: every customer is assumed to be a criminal pirate.
- Manufacture may also want to deploy security measures that avoid device cloning. This may also be true for military systems.

All stakeholders are confronted with threats: pirates, thieves, terrorists, dictators, et cetera. The challenge is to find solutions which respect all the needs, not only the needs of one of the stakeholders. Another challenge is to make systems sufficiently secure, where a little bit insecure quickly means entirely insecure. Last but not least is the human factor often the weakest link in the security chain.

Upgradability and Maintenance:-

It is important to consider how embedded system is going to be serviced and maintained in future. Often product is shipped with defects or problems found in the field and there may be situations where it is not easy to ship back product for upgrade so thought should be kept in mind while designing an embedded system on the options to offer that ease up servicing and maintenance, including installation of software patches to fix existing issue or add new features.

To best meet this optimization challenge, the designer must be comfortable with a variety of hardware and software implementation technologies, and must be able to migrate from one technology to another, in order to find the best implementation for a given application and constraints. Thus, a designer cannot simply be a hardware expert or a software expert, as is commonly the case today; the embedded system designer must have good knowledge in both areas.

2. Handling Interrupts

2.1 Introduction

Interrupts are essential feature of an embedded system. They enable the software to respond, in a timely fashion, to internal and external hardware events. By managing the interaction with external systems, effective use of interrupts can dramatically improve system efficiency and the use of processing resources. For example, the reception and transmission of bytes via UART is more efficient using interrupts rather than polling method. By offloading the tasks to the hardware module so as to report back when finished, drastically improves performance.

Interrupts play more critical role in real time systems since the events have to handle in real-time for example synchronization of a video input. This requires low latency and determinism since the action needs to be handled in a particular time-frame. If an inordinate delay occurs the user will perceive the system as being non-responsive.

The chapter describes various type of interrupts as part of interrupt classification with schemes that are more applicable for embedded application. Faster interrupt response being one the key aspects of embedded systems, chapter provides techniques to measure interrupt latency and methods for interrupt processing to keep the latency low and deterministic for a real time embedded system.

2.2 Interrupts

An *"interrupt"* is event triggered inside an embedded device, either by internal or external hardware, that initiates automatic transfer of software execution to an interrupt service routine (ISR). On completion of ISR, software execution returns to the next instruction that would have occurred without the interrupt. The behavior is shown in Figure 2-1.

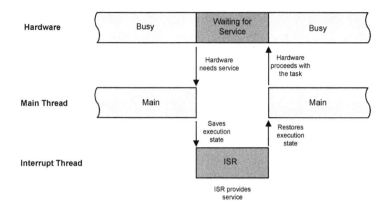

Figure 2-1: Interrupt Service Routine (ISR) flow

A *"thread"* is defined as sequence of instructions that has its own program counter, stack counter, stack and registers; it shares its address space and system resources with other threads. By contrast, a *"process"* has its own virtual address space (stack, data and code) and system resources [1]. Processes are normally used in systems with an operating system, whereas threads are easily implemented in simple embedded systems using interrupt service routines.

2.3 Interrupts versus Polling

When a computer's CPU begins a path of execution without any mechanism of introducing outside input to the system it will continue down the path of execution in a perfectly predictable manner until the computation is complete, or it falls into an infinite loop. The earliest computers worked exactly like this. A user would program an algorithm to process and would wait until computation completed. Embedded systems (as well as Modern computers), however, need the ability to react to and integrate input from outside itself in order to be more responsive, flexible, and easy to use. However, these mechanisms still fall into two general categories:

"Interrupts" and *"Polling"*. The difference between the two is best summed up as:

"Tell me when." versus "I'll ask you."

As an example, consider boiling water on a stove. When using a pot to hold the water, one must check the pot every few minutes to determine if the water is boiling. This is "*Polling*". You regularly need to check the status of the water. A negative consequence of this approach is that if you do not check regularly enough, the pot can boil over and you will not know until the next time you check it. This kind of 'overflow' can happen with polling as well, resulting in lost or corrupt data. Even without lost data, the latency of polling is only as fast as the polling interval which poses problems for some situations.

The alternative to boiling water in a pot would be to use a whistling kettle to let you when the water has reached a boil. The kettle informs you that the water is boiling by signaling you with the whistle. This would be an example of "*Interrupt*".

Generally, the time it takes to get information from your average device, the CPU could be off doing something far more useful than waiting for a busy but slow device. So to keep from having to busy-wait all the time, interrupts are provided which can interrupt whatever is happening so that the operating system can do some task and return to what it was doing without losing information. In an ideal world, all devices would probably work by using interrupts. However, on a PC or clone, there are only a few interrupts available for use by your peripherals, so some drivers have to poll the hardware: ask the hardware if it is ready to transfer data yet. This unfortunately wastes time, but it sometimes needs to be done.

Interrupts in a computer system are often used for guaranteeing that a system has an opportunity to respond to external input immediately, but this can be disadvantageous if the external input happens often, as is often the case with external I/O. An interrupt generally involves the CPU jumping to a new location in code, saving its short-term memory (the registers) and changing other aspects of its internal state so that it can properly respond to the interrupt. This process (or ISR Routine as explained in previous section), takes valuable processing time and if it happens regularly enough can have a serious impact on a system's performance.

In general, Polling uses a lot of CPU horsepower to check whether the peripheral is ready or not, thus inefficient. In comparison, Interrupts use the CPU only when work is done, thus very efficient. All IO in modern computers are interrupt driven.

So both methods have their own advantages and disadvantages. In a modern computer a good example of a polled input is mouse movement. A mouse could produce thousands of interrupts a second, but since the mouse is only updated on screen when the screen refreshes it only makes sense to poll it once every screen refresh (i.e. 60-100 times a second). So a typical desktop PC will delegate the handling of the mouse communication to a subsystem that it checks on a regular basis to determine the current mouse position. This may not be entirely true as the subsystem that manages the mouse is itself interrupt-driven. Another a good example of a system that is both polled and interrupt driven is the PC keyboard. The subsystem that accepts data from the keyboard generally just buffers the data for polling by the CPU but can be programmed to generate interrupts as well. The most famous use of this is the key combination Control-Alt-Delete, which sends a "*non-maskable*" interrupt to the CPU.

Specific to embedded systems, some common examples events that can generate interrupts include: a timer overflows or reaches an assigned value, a serial input device has received a new character, a serial output device is ready to send a new character, an input pin has changed state, the system voltage has dropped below a safe level, or an ADC (analog to digital converter) has finished a new conversion. This list is by no means all-encompassing. In context to an embedded system, operations would be often be interrupt driven as response time and determinism (to be able to respond within specific time) is one of the key aspects of any embedded application.

2.4 Classification of Interrupts

Interrupts are mainly classified into two types:

Synchronous (or Software) Interrupt: A synchronous interrupt is one that will be generated by software that is known to occur at a particular time when a particular instruction gets executed. This is so called because it is predictable, and only occurs when some part of code gets executed in particular context. Some of the common examples for synchronous interrupt include: Divide by Zero, System call, illegal opcode detection, Bad pointer dereference etc.

Asynchronous (or Hardware) Interrupt: An asynchronous interrupt is one that is generated by a hardware device in response to an external event and is unpredictable to the kernel and the user of the instance when a device triggers interrupt and needs attention. Since these are generated at arbitrary time with respect to CPU clock cycles, thus called Asynchronous Interrupts. Common examples include: Interrupt due to Device IO, Timer events etc.

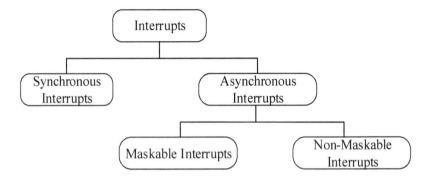

Figure 2-2: Interrupt Classification

Most of the popular microprocessor manuals designate synchronous and asynchronous interrupts as *"Exceptions"* and *"Interrupts"* respectively.

Asynchronous or Hardware interrupts may further be classified into *"Maskable"* or *"Non-maskable"* Interrupts.

Maskable Interrupts: Maskable interrupts are the one that can be blocked by various masking techniques in the hardware.

Non-maskable interrupt (or NMI): Non-maskable interrupts or NMI are the one that are always recognized by the hardware. An NMI generally signals a catastrophic event and is often used when response time is critical or when an interrupt should never be disabled during normal system operation. Such uses include reporting non-recoverable hardware errors, system debugging and profiling, and handling of special cases like system resets.

In modern architectures, NMIs are typically used to handle non-recoverable errors which need immediate attention. Therefore, such interrupts should not be masked in the normal operation of the system. These errors include non-recoverable internal system chipset errors, corruption in system memory such as parity and ECC errors, and data corruption detected on system and peripheral buses.

NMI is used to execute an interrupt handler that transfers control to a specific routine or special monitor program. From this program a developer can inspect the machine's memory, and examine the internal state of the program at the instant of its interruption.

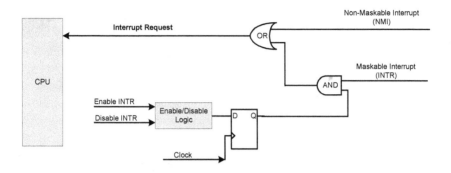

Figure 2-3: Maskable and Non-Maskable Interrupt

Figure 2-3 shows the schematic representation of maskable and non-maskable interrupt.

2.4.1 Vectored and Non-Vectored Interrupts

Another classification is based on whether the interrupts are vector based or non-vector based interrupts.

In Computer world, *"Vectored Interrupts"* are type of I/O interrupts in which the device that generates the interrupt request (also commonly called IRQ) identifies itself directly to the processor. This is in contrast with comparatively inefficient technique of polling, in which the processor polls - looks up - all the I/O devices connected to the interrupt bus.

Vectored interrupts can be achieved by having each I/O device a unique code. When a device generates IRQ, it sends its unique code over the bus to the processor. This code can be the starting address of Interrupt service routine for the I/O device and is typically 4 to 8 bits long [9].

Vectored interrupts requires that the interrupting device supply the CPU with the starting address or transfer vector of ISR while *"Non-vectored interrupts"* has pre-fixed start address of the ISRs.

Non-vectored interrupts are very useful for embedded systems or small systems where there are few interrupt sources and the software structure is straightforward. So the easiest way to service interrupts in a system is by having the interrupt request lines through a single multi-drop interrupt request line shown as "*IRQ*" in Figure 2-4.

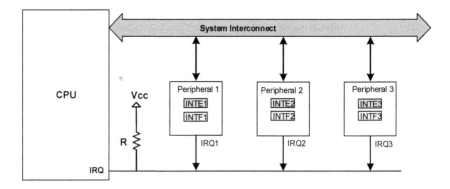

Figure 2-4: Managing Non-vectored interrupts

When either of the peripherals places request, IRQ line to the CPU gets asserted, triggering a request. However this does not let CPU identify actual source of interrupt between Peripheral 1, Peripheral 2 or Peripheral 3, so within the ISR CPU proceeds to check the service request flags (denoted by "*INTF*") of all the peripherals to find out who placed the request. Each peripheral has open drain request line tied to the processor *IRQ* line. The activation of interrupt request by a particular peripheral will set its interrupt Flag *INTF*. If the peripheral interrupt is enabled (denote by *INTE*), its *IRQ* will be asserted, placing a request to the CPU. Interrupt will take place by loading the PC with a pre-defined address where ISR is stored. The ISR address in a non-vectored systems is usually fixed to a certain location in the program memory where the ISR must be stored in order to be executed. When any peripheral places a request, a single ISR is executed and code within the ISR polls the interrupt flag *INF* of each peripheral to determine who placed the request. The absence of hardware mechanism allowing the CPU automatically identifying who placed the service request is what gains the method the name "*Non-Vectored*" [10]. Some of the processor that support Non-vectored interrupts include 8085, 6802, PowerPC, MIPS and MSP430.

Vectored interrupts is rather based on interrupt vector description table (IDT).During an interrupt acknowledge cycle a vector is supplied which is used to point to an entry in the interrupt vector table. The entry is the start address of the ISR and it is automatically loaded into the processor's program counter. The vector table contents are loaded by software.

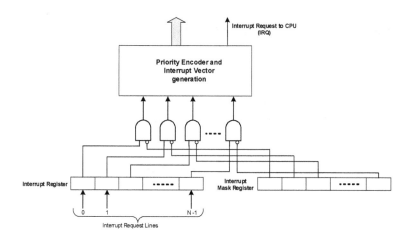

Figure 2-5: A vectored interrupt scheme

For the MC68000 and 8086 the vector table is in a fixed position in the memory map [11]. In the Z8000 and Z80, however, the position of the table is relative to the contents of an internal register. An 8-bit vector allows for 256 entries in the vector table. The 8086 predefines or reserves 32 of these and care must be taken to avoid generating these vectors externally. For MC68000, Z8000 and Z80, the full range is available for user definition [11].

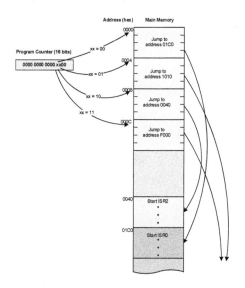

Figure 2-6: A vectored interrupt scheme with interrupt vector description table

2.5 Interrupt Service Routine (ISR), Interrupt Vectors and Vector Table

The CPU must know where to fetch the next instruction following an interrupt. The address of an ISR is defined in an *"Interrupt vector"*. Most popular microcontroller's uses vectored interrupts where each ISR has its own vector stored in a *"Vector table"* located at either the beginning or end of the program memory.

Most common processors include a Vector table that defines the start address of interrupt service routine.

Some processors uses *"predefined"* approach (Atmel AVR, 8051 and Microchip) where Program Counter (PC) is loaded with a predefined address of some entry within the IVT. Usually each entry is a JUMP address to the address of the interrupt service routine (ISR) for that interrupt.

An alternate method (commonly known as *"fetch"*) loads the PC indirectly using the address of some entry inside the IVT to pull an address out of that table, and then loading the PC with that address. Fetch method is common in Motorola/Freescale Microcontrollers.

Figure 2-7 shows typical memory map organization for a microcontroller, showing the location of Interrupt Vectors or Interrupt Vector Table (IVT) that include the JUMP address to the ISR for the particular interrupt vector.

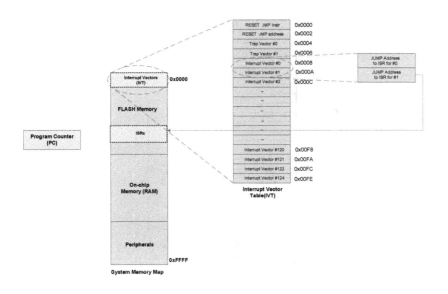

Figure 2-7: Location on Interrupt Vectors in typical Memory Map

NOTE: *The vector table is at a fixed location (defined by the processor data sheet), but the ISRs can be located anywhere in memory.*

2.5.1 Example: Microchip dsPIC33F Digital Signal Controller IVT

Figure 2-8 and Figure 2-9 shows the Interrupt Vector Table (IVT) and the Interrupt Vectors (only first 32 interrupt vectors shown) for Microchip dsPIC33F Digital Signal Controllers [12] .

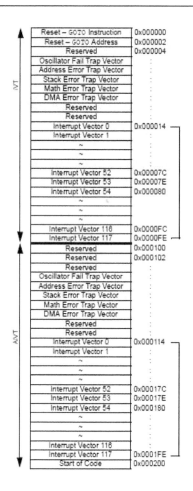

Figure 2-8: Microchip dsPIC33F Interrupt Vector Table (IVT)[1]

dsPIC33F Interrupt Vector Table (IVT) resides in program memory starting at location 0x000004. The IVT contains 126 vectors consisting of eight non-maskable trap vectors and up to 118 sources of interrupt. In general, each interrupt source has its own vector. Each interrupt vector contains a 24-bit wide address. The value programmed into each interrupt

---

[1] Microchip dsPIC33F Interrupt Vector Table reprinted with permission of the copyright owner, Microchip Technology Incorporated. All rights reserved. No further reprints or reproductions may be made without Microchip Technology Inc.'s prior written consent.

vector location is the starting address of the associated Interrupt Service Route (ISR).

One may also notice that dsPIC33F includes Alternate Interrupt Vector Table (AIVT) in the memory map providing means to switch between an application and a support environment without requiring the interrupt vectors to be reprogrammed. Based on ALTIVT bit in Interrupt control register all interrupt and exception processes use either the default vectors or alternate vectors.

Vector Number	IVT Address	AIVT Address	Interrupt Source
0	0x000004	0x000104	Reserved
1	0x000006	0x000106	Oscillator Failure
2	0x000008	0x000108	Address Error
3	0x00000A	0x00010A	Stack Error
4	0x00000C	0x00010C	Math Error
5	0x00000E	0x00010E	DMA Error
6	0x000010	0x000110	Reserved
7	0x000012	0x000112	Reserved
8	0x000014	0x000114	INT0 – External Interrupt 0
9	0x000016	0x000116	IC1 – Input Capture 1
10	0x000018	0x000118	OC1 – Output Compare 1
11	0x00001A	0x00011A	T1 – Timer1
12	0x00001C	0x00011C	DMA0 – DMA Channel 0
13	0x00001E	0x00011E	IC2 – Input Capture 2
14	0x000020	0x000120	OC2 – Output Compare 2
15	0x000022	0x000122	T2 – Timer2
16	0x000024	0x000124	T3 – Timer3
17	0x000026	0x000126	SPI1E – SPI1 Error
18	0x000028	0x000128	SPI1 – SPI1 Transfer Done
19	0x00002A	0x00012A	U1RX – UART1 Receiver
20	0x00002C	0x00012C	U1TX – UART1 Transmitter
21	0x00002E	0x00012E	AD1 – ADC1 Convert Done
22	0x000030	0x000130	DMA1 – DMA Channel 1
23	0x000032	0x000132	Reserved
24	0x000034	0x000134	SI2C1 – I²C™1 Slave Events
25	0x000036	0x000136	MI2C1 – I²C1 Master Events
26	0x000038	0x000138	CMP – Comparator Interrupt
27	0x00003A	0x00013A	CN – Change Notification Interrupt
28	0x00003C	0x00013C	INT1 – External Interrupt 1
29	0x00003E	0x00013E	Reserved
30	0x000040	0x000140	IC7 – Input Capture 7
31	0x000042	0x000142	IC8 – Input Capture 8
32	0x000044	0x000144	DMA2 – DMA Channel 2

Figure 2-9: Microchip dsPIC33F Interrupt Vectors[2]

Also note that for dsPIC33F, Interrupt controller is not involved in reset process. The dsPIC33F device clears its registers in response to a Reset, which forces the Program Counter (PC) to zero. The processor then starts

---

[2] Microchip dsPIC33F Interrupt Vector Table reprinted with permission of the copyright owner, Microchip Technology Incorporated. All rights reserved. No further reprints or reproductions may be made without Microchip Technology Inc.'s prior written consent.

program execution at location 0x000000. The user application programs a GOTO instruction at the Reset address, which redirects program execution to the appropriate start-up routine.

2.5.2 Example: Freescale Kinetis Microcontroller IVT

Kinetis KL25 is based on ARM Cortex™ M0+ that include Nested Vector Interrupt Controller (NVIC). On the ARMv6-M based architecture NVIC supports up-to 32 external interrupts with 4 different priority levels. This is explained in more details in Section 2.8.1.

The use of an NVIC in the microcontroller profiles means that the vector table is very different from other ARM processors consisting of addresses not instructions. The initial stack pointer and the address of the reset handler must be located at 0x0 and 0x4 respectively. These addresses are loaded into the SP and PC registers by the processor at reset.

Address	Vector	IRQ[1]	NVIC IPR register number[2]	Source module	Source description
0x0000_0000	0	—	—	ARM core	Initial Stack Pointer
0x0000_0004	1	—	—	ARM core	Initial Program Counter
0x0000_0008	2	—	—	ARM core	Non-maskable Interrupt (NMI)
0x0000_000C	3	—	—	ARM core	Hard Fault
0x0000_0010	4	—	—	—	—
0x0000_0014	5	—	—	—	—
0x0000_0018	6	—	—	—	—
0x0000_001C	7	—	—	—	—
0x0000_0020	8	—	—	—	—
0x0000_0024	9	—	—	—	—
0x0000_0028	10	—	—	—	—
0x0000_002C	11	—	—	ARM core	Supervisor call (SVCall)
0x0000_0030	12	—	—	—	—
0x0000_0034	13	—	—	—	—
0x0000_0038	14	—	—	ARM core	Pendable request for system service (PendableSrvReq)
0x0000_003C	15	—	—	ARM core	System tick timer (SysTick)
Non-Core Vectors					
0x0000_0040	16	0	0	DMA	DMA channel 0 transfer complete and error
0x0000_0044	17	1	0	DMA	DMA channel 1 transfer complete and error
0x0000_0048	18	2	0	DMA	DMA channel 2 transfer complete and error
0x0000_004C	19	3	0	DMA	DMA channel 3 transfer complete and error
0x0000_0050	20	4	1	—	—
0x0000_0054	21	5	1	FTFA	Command complete and read collision
0x0000_0058	22	6	1	PMC	Low-voltage detect, low-voltage warning
0x0000_005C	23	7	1	LLWU	Low Leakage Wakeup
0x0000_0060	24	8	2	I²C0	
0x0000_0064	25	9	2	I²C1	
0x0000_0068	26	10	2	SPI0	Single interrupt vector for all sources
0x0000_006C	27	11	2	SPI1	Single interrupt vector for all sources
0x0000_0070	28	12	3	UART0	Status and error
0x0000_0074	29	13	3	UART1	Status and error
0x0000_0078	30	14	3	UART2	Status and error
0x0000_007C	31	15	3	ADC0	
0x0000_0080	32	16	4	CMP0	
0x0000_0084	33	17	4	TPM0	
0x0000_0088	34	18	4	TPM1	
0x0000_008C	35	19	4	TPM2	

Figure 2-10: Snapshot of Kinetis KL25 Interrupt vector assignments[3]

2.6 Interrupt Processing

When an interrupt occurs, the following sequence is followed:-

1. The execution of main program is suspended by the hardware.
   - Current instruction is still allowed to be finished
   - All the registers are pushed onto the stack

[3] Copyright Freescale Semiconductor (http://freescale.com). Used by Permission

- Vector address is retrieved from the memory and placed in the PC.
- Generally any other interrupts will be optionally disabled by programming particular interrupt mask bits.

2. The Interrupt service routine (ISR) is executed. ISR includes
   - Performs the necessary operation for the specific interrupt
   - Clears the interrupt flag

3. ISR executes Return from Interrupt (RTI) Instruction to resume the main program
   - Hardware pulls all the registers from the stack
   - This includes the Program Counter (PC) to resume from the point where it was interrupted.

Figure 2-11 shows the flow diagram for interrupt processing.

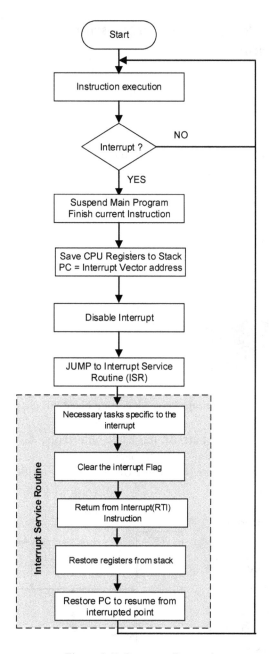

Figure 2-11: Interrupt Processing

2.6.1 Example: Interrupt Processing using Fixed ISR Location

Figure 2-12 shows an example of interrupt processing using Fixed ISR location.

STEP 1: CPU executes its main program that includes series of instructions. While executing instruction at 100, P1 receives input data in the register with address 0x2000 and asserts *"Int"* to request servicing by the CPU.

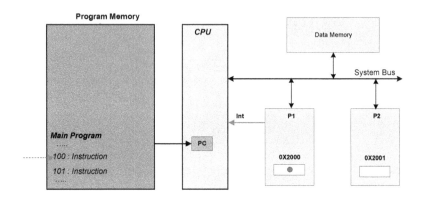

Figure 2-12: Interrupt Processing using Fixed ISR (Step 1)

STEP 2: Since *"Int"* is part of maskable interrupts, CPU waits until completion of Instruction at 0x100 to begin processing the interrupt. CPU saves the Program Counter (PC) value of 0x100 and sets PC to ISR fixed location at 0x10.

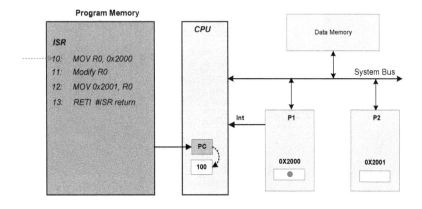

Figure 2-13: Interrupt Processing using Fixed ISR (Step 2)

STEP 3: The ISR reads data from 0x2000, modifies the data and writes the resulting data in 0x2001 (as shown). Once the data from P1 is read, it deasserts *"Int"*.

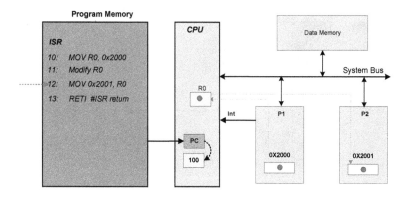

Figure 2-14: Interrupt Processing using Fixed ISR (Step 3)

STEP 4: ISR ends with a return (or RETI) instruction, thereby restoring PC to 100+1 =101 where CPU resumes executing next instruction.

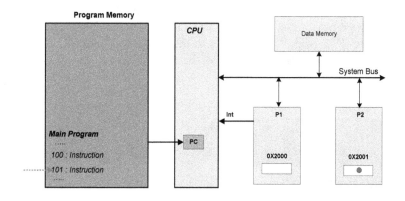

Figure 2-15: Interrupt Processing using Fixed ISR (Step 4)

2.6.2 Example: Interrupt Processing using Vectored Interrupt

Figure 2-16 shows an example of interrupt processing using Vectored interrupt.

STEP 1: CPU executes its main program that includes series of instructions. While executing instruction at 100, P1 receives input data in the register with address 0x2000 and asserts "*Int*" to request servicing by the CPU.

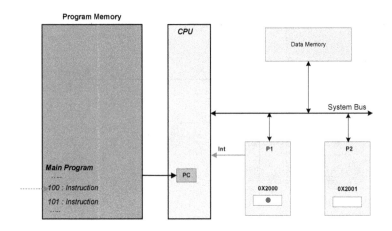

Figure 2-16: Interrupt Processing using Vectored Interrupts (Step 1)

STEP 2: Since "*Int*" is part of maskable interrupts, CPU waits until completion of Instruction at 0x100 to begin processing the interrupt. CPU saves the Program Counter (PC) value of 0x100 and accesses the Interrupt Vector Table (IVT) with "*Int*" as offset to the IVT to get back the address of the ISR location. It then sets PC to the ISR address location fetched from IVT.

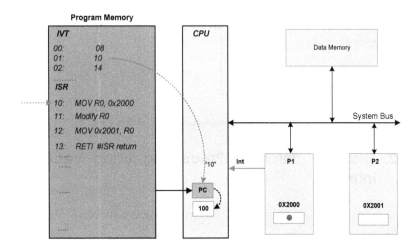

Figure 2-17: Interrupt Processing using Vectored Interrupts (Step 2)

STEP 3: The ISR reads data from 0x2000, modifies the data and writes the resulting data in 0x2001 (as shown). Once the data from P1 is read, it deasserts *"Int".*

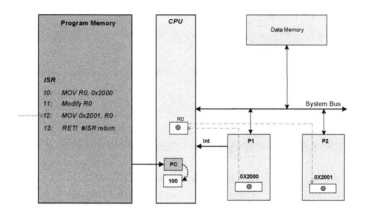

Figure 2-18: Interrupt Processing using Vectored Interrupts (Step 3)

STEP 4: ISR ends with a return (or RETI) instruction, thereby restoring PC to 100+1 =101 where CPU resumes executing next instruction.

2.7 Interrupt Latency

Interrupt latency is one of the key characteristics of an embedded system. For certain applications with real time requirements, this is very critical parameter.

The term interrupt latency refers to the number of clock cycles required for a processor to responds to an interrupt request, this is typically a measure based on the number of clock cycles between the assertion of the interrupt request up to the cycle where the first instruction of the interrupt handler exited [13].

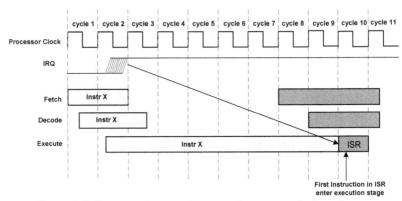

Figure 2-19: Interrupt Latency in terms of processor clock cycles

In many cases, when the clock frequency of the system is known, the interrupt latency can also be expressed in terms of time delay, for example, in μsec.

For generic processors, the exact interrupt latency depends on what the processor is executing at the time the interrupt occurs. For example, in many processor architectures, the processor starts to respond to an interrupt request only when the current executing instruction completes, which can add a number of extra clock cycles. Therefore the maximum latency from interrupt request to completion of the hardware response consists of the execution time of the slowest instruction plus the time required to complete the memory transfers required by the hardware response.

As a result, the interrupt latency value can contain a best case and a worst case value. This variation can results in jitters of interrupt responses, which could be problematic in certain applications like audio processing (with the introduction of signal distortions) and motor control (which can result in harmonics or vibrations) [13].

2.7.1 Measuring Interrupt Latency

Assume a simple application using real-time interrupt to generate pulses on SoC output pins, "*OUT[1:0]*" (the pulses on these particular output pins could be used to keep track of the elapsed time by an external counter, or for viewing interrupt processing time on the oscilloscope, for example)

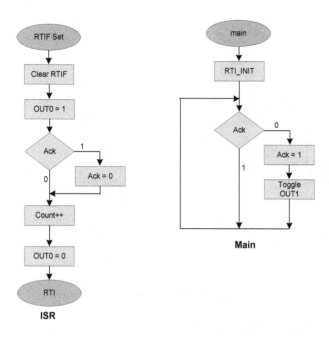

Figure 2-20: Measuring Interrupt Latency

2.7.2 Example: Serial Communication using interrupts

Consider a common case for the application that uses the serial communication interface (UART). The UART hardware receives characters at an asynchronous rate. In order to avoid loss of data in periods of high activity, characters need to be stored in a FIFO buffer. The main program can process characters at a rate which is independent of the rate at which the characters arrive. It must process the characters at an average rate which is faster than the average rate at which they can arrive, otherwise the FIFO buffer will become full and data will be lost. In other words, buffer allows the input data to arrive in bursts, and the main program can access them when it is ready.

The following figure shows the situation of character reception.

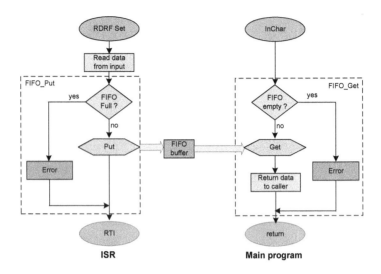

Figure 2-21: Interrupt Driven Input Routine

The structure for interrupt-driven character transmission is similar, except that the output device interrupt requests could be implemented in two different ways - those that request an interrupt on the transmission to the ready state and those that request an interrupt when they are *in* the ready state. This section only provides details for the former as an example.

For transmission, output device requests an interrupt when it finishes processing the current output to indicate that it is now ready for the next output. In other words, output ISR is invoked only when the output device transitions from a *"busy"* condition to *"ready"* condition. In the context to serial transmission, this creates two problems:-

- When the main program(aka background thread) puts the first byte in the FIFO buffer, the output device is idle and already in *"ready"* state, so no interrupt request from the output device is about to occur. The output ISR will not be invoked and the data will not be removed be removed from the buffer.
- If somehow started, the interrupt *"FIFO_get"* output cycle will repeat as long as there is data in the buffer. However if the output ever becomes ready when the buffer is empty, no subsequent interrupt will occur to remove the next byte place in the buffer.

54

In these situations, hardware normally provides a mechanism to determine whether or not the output device is busy processing the data, such as flags in status registers. In this cases, main work of the ISR should be placed in separate function (e.g SendData) that actually outputs the data.

The main program (background thread in this case) checks the output busy flag every time it writes data to the buffer. If the device is busy, then a device ready interrupt is expected and nothing needs to be done otherwise the background thread *arms* the output and calls *SendData* to "*kick start*" the output process.

The *SendData* routine is responsible for retrieving the data from the buffer and outputting it. If there is no more data in the buffer, then it must *disarm* the output to prevent further interrupts.

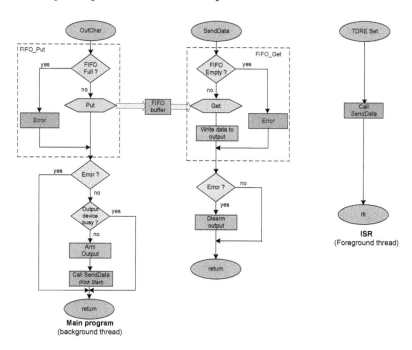

Figure 2-22: Kick Start an interrupt-driven output routine for a device that requests interrupts on transitioning from busy to ready

2.8 Latency for Embedded Systems

For an input device, the interface latency is the time between when new input is available, and the time when the software reads the input data. We can also define device latency as the response time of the external I/O device. For example, if we request that a certain sector be read from a disk, then the device latency is the time it take to find the correct track and spin the disk (seek) so the proper sector is positioned under the read head. For an output device, the interface latency is the time between when the output device is idle, and the time when the software writes new data. A real-time system is one that can guarantee worst case interface latency.

Many factors should be considered when deciding the most appropriate mechanism to synchronize hardware and software. One should avoid using *"busy wait"* unless it's a simple system. Busy-wait synchronization is appropriate when the I/O timing is predictable and when the I/O structure is simple and fixed. Busy wait should be used for dedicated single thread systems where there is nothing else to do while the I/O is busy. Interrupt synchronization is appropriate when the I/O timing is variable, and when the I/O structure is complex. In particular, interrupts are efficient when there are I/O devices with different speeds. Interrupts allow for quick response times to important events. In particular, using interrupts is one mechanism to design real-time systems, where the interface latency must be *short* and *bounded*. *Bounded* means it is always less than a specified value. *Short* means the specified value is acceptable to our consumers [14].

2.8.1 Interrupt Latency of ARM Cortex®-M Processors and NVIC

The Nested Vector Interrupt Controller (NVIC) in the Cortex-M processor family is an example of an interrupt controller with extremely flexible interrupt priority management. It enables programmable priority levels, automatic nested interrupt support, along with support for multiple interrupt masking.

For the Cortex-M0 and Cortex-M0+ processors, the NVIC design supports up to 32 interrupt inputs plus a number of built-in system exceptions [13](Figure 2-23). For each interrupt input, there are 4 programmable priority levels (Figure 2-24). Higher Cortex-M processors supports larger number of interrupt inputs. In practice the number of interrupt inputs and the number of priority levels are likely to be driven by the application requirements, and defined by silicon designers based on the needs of the chip design.

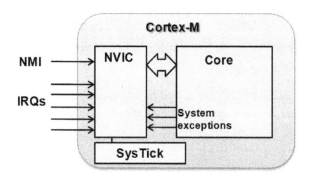

Figure 2-23: NVIC on ARM Cortex-M Processor[4] [13]

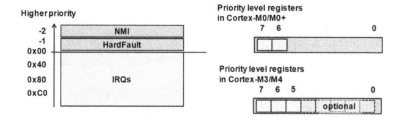

Figure 2-24: Programmable Priority Level on ARM Cortex-M Processors[5] [13]

In addition to the interrupt requests from peripherals, the NVIC design supports internal exceptions, for example, an exception input from a 24-bit timer call SysTick, which is often used by the OS. There are also additional system exceptions to support OS operations, and a Non-Maskable Interrupt (NMI) input. The NMI and HardFault (one of the system exceptions) have fixed priority levels.

For a zero wait state memory systems, following table shows the latency in terms of number of clock cycles from time when interrupt request is asserted to the time when the first instruction of the interrupt handler is ready to be executed.

---

[4] *Reproduced with permission from ARM Limited. Copyright © ARM Limited*

Processors	# Clock Cycles
Cortex-M0	16
Cortex-M0+	15
Cortex-M3	12
Cortex-M4	12

Table 2-1: Interrupt latency of ARM Cortex-M Processors [13]

The above latency numbers is based on following assumptions:-

- The memory system has zero wait states
- The system level design of the chip does not add delay in the interrupt signal connections between the interrupt sources and the processor
- The Interrupt service is not blocked by another current running exception/interrupt service
- For Cortex-M4, with FPU enabled, the lazy stacking feature is enabled (this is the default) [13]
- The current executing instruction is not doing an unaligned transfer/bit band transfer (which can take 1 extra transfer cycle)

To make the Cortex-M devices easy to use and program, and to support the automatic handling of nested exceptions or interrupts, the interrupt response sequence includes a number of stack push operations. This enables all of the interrupt handlers to be written as normal C subroutines, and enables the ISR to start real work immediately without the need to spend time on saving current context.

Just considering the processor interrupt latency may not provide overall interrupt response time. One must consider software overhead to handle the interrupts (like stacking of registers, switching register bank, check the actual interrupt source if it is shared interrupt and other misc. tasks).

As in any program code, ISRs take time to execute. The faster the performance of the processor, the quicker the interrupt request is serviced, and the longer the system can stay in sleep mode thus reducing power consumption. When considering from the time an interrupt request is asserted to the time the interrupt processing is actually completed, the Cortex-M processors claims to be better than other microcontrollers due to lower software overheads.

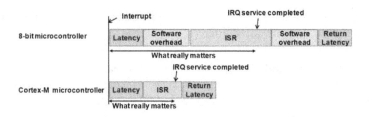

Figure 2-25: Cortex-M versus 8-bit 8051 processor[5] [13]

In traditional 8-bit/16-bit systems, the run time for ISRs can be many more cycles than with Cortex-M based microcontrollers because of lower performance. When combined with the higher maximum clock speed of many Cortex-M based microcontrollers, the maximum interrupt processing capacity can be much higher than other microcontroller products [13].

2.8.2 Interrupt Response Jitter

The jitter of interrupt response time refers to the variation (or value range) of interrupt latency cycles. In many systems, the interrupt latency cycle depends on what the CPU is doing when the interrupt takes place. For example, in an architecture like the 8051, if the processor is executing a multi-cycle instruction, the interrupt entry sequence cannot start until the instruction is finished, which can be a few cycles later. This results in a variation of the number of interrupt latency cycles, and is commonly referred as jitter.

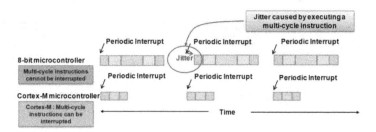

Figure 2-26: Interrupt Jitter Response[5] [13]

In most general purpose applications the jitter doesn't matter. However, in real time applications that needs determinism, like audio or motor control,

---

[5] *Reproduced with permission from ARM Limited. Copyright © ARM Limited*

the jitter can results in distortion of audio signals, or vibration/noise of motors due to this unwanted jitter.

In some of the embedded processor targeted for real time operating system (Like Cortex-M processors) , if a multiple cycle instruction is being executed when an interrupt arrives, in most cases, the instruction is abandoned and restarted when the ISR is completed. On ARM Cortex-M3 [13] processor if the interrupt request is received during a multiple load/store (memory access) instruction, the current state of the multiple transfer is automatically stored as part of the PSR (Program Status Register) and when the ISR completes, the multiple transfer can resume from where it was stalled by using the saved information in the PSR. This mechanism provides high performance processing while at the same time maintains low jitter in the interrupt response time.

ARM Cortex-M3 [13] also includes *"Tail Chaining"* – technique that allows processor to switch to pending ISR after the current ISR is complete by skipping some of the un-stacking and stacking operations which are normally needed(see Figure 2-27). This also makes the processor much more energy efficient by avoiding unnecessary memory accesses.

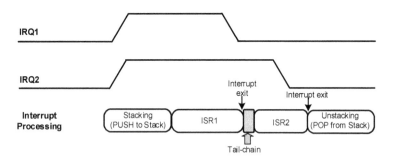

Figure 2-27: ARM Cortex-M3[4] Tail Chaining[6] [13]

---

[6] *Reproduced with permission from ARM Limited. Copyright © ARM Limited*

3. Memory Addressing

3.1 Introduction

Many type of memory devices are used in an embedded system. Architect and designers focused on embedded systems must be aware of the differences between them and understand how to use each type effectively. This chapter covers all about memories in context to embedded systems. First few sections covers the memory technologies and memory classification based on various characteristics. Later sections focus on building memory system using memory devices and combinational components for an efficient memory system design.

Any well designed embedded system will use a variety of memories, essentially building a memory hierarchy allowing designers to treat system design as a modularized process, to treat the memory system as an abstraction and to optimize individual subsystems. Section on *"Memory hierarchy"* provides various tradeoff in context to latency, bandwidth and cost per bit in building up efficient memory hierarchy best suited for specific embedded application. Later sections also include *"Endianness"* considerations in context to embedded systems. Endianness describes how multi-byte data is represented by an embedded system. The difference in Endian-architecture is an issue when software or data is shared between systems unless all embedded systems are designed with same Endian-architecture, which is specifically true for Internet of Things (IoT) that requires devices from different manufactures, with different operating system to work together without any restrictions. To have efficient data transfers between the devices with lowest latency requires Endianness to be kept in mind while architecting an embedded system.

3.2 Memory Classification

Memory Devices can be classified based on following characteristics

- Accessibility
- Persistence of Storage
- Storage Density & Cost

- Storage Media
- Power Consumption

Accessibility

Memory devices can provide Random Access, Serial Access or Block Access. In a Random Access memory, each word in memory can be directly accessed by specifying the address of the memory word. RAM, SDRAMs, and NOR Flash are examples of Random Access Memories. In a Serial Access Memory, all the previous words (previous to the word being accessed) need to be accessed, before accessing a desired word. I2C PROM and SPI PROM are examples of Serial Access Memories. In Block Access Memories, entire memory is sub-divided in to small blocks (generally of the order of a Kbyte) of memory. Each block can be randomly accessed, and each word in a given block can be serially accessed. Hard Disks and NAND flash employ a similar mechanism. Word access time for a *RAM* (Random Access Memory) is independent of the word location. This is desirable of high speed application making frequent access to the memory.

Persistence of Storage

Memory devices can provide Volatile storage or a non-Volatile storage. In a non-Volatile storage, the memory contents remain preserved even after power shut down whereas a Volatile memory loses its contents, after power shut down. Non-Volatile storage can be used to store application code, and re-usable data while volatile memory can be used for all temporary storage. RAM, SDRAM are examples of volatile memory. Hard Disks, Flash (NOR & NAND) Memories, SD-MMC, and ROM are example of non-Volatile storages.

Storage Cells

Memory Device may employ electronic (in terms of transistors or electron states) storage, magnetic storage or optical storage. RAM, SDRAM are examples of electronic storage. Hard Disks are example of magnetic storage. CDs (Compact Discs) are example of optical storage. Legacy computers also employed magnetic storage (magnetic storages are still common in some consumer electronics products).

Storage Density & Cost

Storage Density (number of bits which can be stored per unit area) is generally a good measure of cost. Dense memories (like SDRAM) are much cheaper than their counterparts (like SRAM)

Power Consumption

Low Power Consumption is highly desirable in Battery Powered Embedded Systems. Such systems generally employ memory devices which can operate at low (and ultra-low) Voltage levels. Mobile SDRAMs are example of low power memories.

3.3 Memory Technologies

Another level of classification would be based on memory technologies.

RAM

RAM stands for Random Access Memory. RAMs are simplest and most common form of volatile data storage. The number of words which can be stored in a RAM are proportional (exponential of two) to the number of address buses available. This severely restricts the storage capacity of RAMs (A 32 GB RAM will require 36 Address lines) because designing circuit boards with more signal lines directly adds to the complexity and cost.

DPRAM (Dual Port RAM)

DPRAM are static RAMs with two I/O ports. These two ports access the same memory locations - hence DPRAMs are generally used to implement Shared Memories in Dual Processor Systems. The operations performed on a single port are identical to any RAM. There are some common problems associated with usage of DPRAM:

(a) Possible of data corruption when both ports are trying to access the same memory location - Most DPRAM devices provide interlocked memory accesses to avoid this problem.

(b) Data Coherency when Cache scheme is being used by the processor accessing DPRAM - This happens because any data modifications (in the DPRAM) by one processor are unknown to the Cache controller of other processor. In order to avoid such issues, Shared memories are not mapped to the Cacheable space. In case processor's cache configuration is not flexible enough (to define the shared memory space as non-cacheable), the cache needs to be flushed before performing any reads from this memory space.

Dynamic RAM

Dynamic RAMs use a different storage technique for data storage. A Static RAM has four transistors per memory cell, whereas Dynamic RAMs have only one transistor per memory cell. The DRAMs use capacitive storage. Since the capacitor can lose charge, these memories need to be refreshed periodically making DRAMs more complex (due to additional control) and power consuming. However, DRAMs have a very high storage density (as compared to static RAMs) and are much cheaper in cost. DRAMs are generally accessed in terms of rows, columns and pages which significantly reduces the number of address buses (another advantage over RAM). Generally SDRAM controller (which manages different SDRAM commands and Address translation) is required to access a SDRAM. Most of the modern processors come with an on-chip SDRAM controller.

OTP- EPROM, UV-EPROM and EEPROM

EPROMs (Electrically Programmable writable Read Only Memory) are non-volatile memories. Contents of ROM can be randomly accessed - but generally the word RAM is used to refer to only the volatile random access memories. The operating voltage for writing in to the EPROMs is much higher thus often need special programming stations (which have write mechanism) to write in to the EPROMs.

OTP-EPROMs are One Time Programmable. Contents of these memories cannot be changed, once written. UV-EPROM are UV erasable EPROMs. Exposure of memory cells, to UV light erases the existing contents of these memories and these can be re-programmed after that. EEPROM are Electrically Erasable EPROMs and can be erased electrically. The endurance cycle (number of times the memory can written) for UV-EPROM and EEPROM is fairly limited. Erasable PROMs use either FLOTOX (Floating gate Tunnel Oxide) or FAMOS (Floating gate Avalanche MOS) technology.

Flash (NOR)

Flash (or NOR-Flash to be more accurate) are quite similar to EEPROM in usage and can be considered in the class of EEPROM (since it is electrically erasable). However there are a few differences. Firstly, the flash devices are in-circuit programmable. Secondly, these are much cheaper as compared to the conventional EEPROMs. NOR Flash are very popular as the main code/boot memory,

NAND FLASH

These memories are denser and cheaper than NOR Flash. However these memories are block accessible, and cannot be used for code execution. These devices are mostly used for Data Storage (being generally cheaper than NOR flash). However some systems use them for storing the boot codes (these can be used with external hardware or with built-in NAND boot logic in the processor).

SD-MMC

SD-MMC cards provide a cheaper mean of mass storage. These memory cards can provide storage capacity of the order of GBytes. These cards are very compact and can be used with portable systems. Most modern hand-held devices requiring mass storage (e.g. still and video cameras) use Memory cards for storage.

Hard Disc

Hard Discs are Optical Memory devices. These devices are bulky and they require another bulky hardware (disk reader) for reading these memories. These memories are generally used for Mass storage. Hence they memories do not exist in smaller and portable systems. However these memories are being used in embedded systems which require bulk storage without any size constraint.

3.4 Memory Classification

Many types of memory devices are available for use in embedded systems. The names of the memory types frequently reflect the historical nature of the development process and are often more confusing than insightful. Figure 3-1 classifies the memory devices particularly in context to embedded systems.

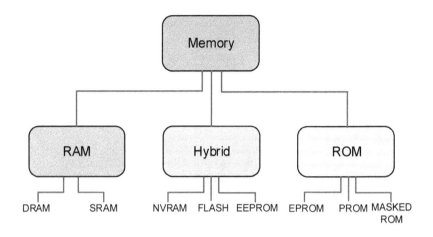

Figure 3-1: Embedded Systems Memory Classification

3.4.1 RAM Classification

The RAM family includes two important memory devices: static RAM (SRAM) and dynamic RAM (DRAM). The primary difference between them is the lifetime of the data they store. SRAM retains its contents as long as electrical power is applied to the chip. If the power is turned off or lost temporarily, its contents will be lost forever. DRAM, on the other hand, has an extremely short data lifetime-typically about few milliseconds. This is true even when power is applied constantly.

In short, SRAM has all the properties of the memory of RAM. Compared to that, DRAM seems kind of useless. By itself, it is. However, a simple piece of hardware called a DRAM controller can be used to make DRAM behave more like SRAM. The job of the DRAM controller is to periodically refresh the data stored in the DRAM. By refreshing the data before it expires, the contents of memory can be kept alive for as long as they are needed.

When deciding which type of RAM to use, a system designer must consider access time and cost. SRAM devices offer extremely fast access times but are much more expensive to produce. Generally, SRAM is used only where access speed is extremely important. A lower cost-per-byte makes DRAM attractive whenever large amounts of RAM are required. Many embedded systems include both types: a small block of SRAM (a few kilobytes) along a critical data path and a much larger block of DRAM (perhaps even Megabytes) for everything else.

3.4.2 ROM Classification

Memories in the ROM family are distinguished by the methods used to write new data (usually called programming), and the number of times they can be rewritten. This classification reflects the evolution of ROM devices from hardwired to programmable to erasable-and-programmable. A common feature of all these devices is their ability to retain data and programs forever, even during a power failure.

The very first ROMs were hardwired devices that contained a preprogrammed set of data or instructions. The contents of the ROM had to be specified before chip production, so the actual data could be used to arrange the transistors inside the chip. Hardwired memories are still used, though they are now called "*Masked ROMs*" to distinguish them from other types of ROM. The primary advantage of a masked ROM is its low production cost. Unfortunately, the cost is low only when large quantities of the same ROM are required.

One step up from the masked ROM is the PROM (programmable ROM), which comes in an unprogrammed state. Data in PROM in an unprogrammed state is made up entirely of 1's. The process of writing data to the PROM involves a special piece of equipment called a device programmer. The device programmer writes data to the device one word at a time by applying an electrical charge to the input pins of the chip. Once a PROM has been programmed in this way, its contents can never be changed. If the code or data stored in the PROM must be changed, the current device must be discarded. As a result, PROMs are also known as one-time programmable (OTP) devices.

An EPROM (erasable-and-programmable ROM) is programmed in exactly the same manner as a PROM. However, EPROMs can be erased and reprogrammed repeatedly. Erasing an EPROM simply requires exposure of the device to a strong source of ultraviolet light. (A window in the top of the device allows the light to reach the silicon.) Doing this essentially resets the entire chip to its initial unprogrammed state. Though more expensive than PROMs, their ability to be reprogrammed makes EPROMs an essential part of the software development and testing process.

3.4.3 Hybrid Memory Classification

As memory technology has matured in recent years, the line between RAM and ROM has blurred. Now, several types of memory combine features of both. These devices do not belong to either group and can be collectively referred to as hybrid memory devices. Hybrid memories can be read and written as desired, like RAM, but maintain their contents without electrical power, just like ROM. Two of the hybrid devices, EEPROM and flash, are descendants of ROM devices. These are typically used to store code. The third hybrid, NVRAM, is a modified version of SRAM. NVRAM usually holds persistent data.

EEPROMs are electrically-erasable-and-programmable. Internally, they are similar to EPROMs, but the erase operation is accomplished electrically, rather than by exposure to ultraviolet light. Any byte within an EEPROM may be erased and rewritten. Once written, the new data will remain in the device until it is electrically erased. The primary tradeoff for this improved functionality is higher cost, though write cycles are also significantly longer than writes to a RAM, one of the reasons for not using an EEPROM for main system memory.

Flash memory combines the best features of the memory devices described thus far. Flash memory devices are high density, low cost, nonvolatile, fast (to read, but not to write), and electrically reprogrammable. Thus Flash offers significant advantages and, as a direct result, the use of flash memory has increased dramatically in embedded systems. From a software viewpoint, flash and EEPROM technologies are very similar. The major difference being that flash devices can only be erased one sector at a time, rather than byte-by-byte. Typical sector sizes are in the range 256 bytes to 16KB. Despite this disadvantage, flash is much more popular than EEPROM and is rapidly displacing many of the ROM devices as well.

The third member of the hybrid memory class includes NVRAM (non-volatile RAM). Non-volatility is also a characteristic of the ROM and hybrid memories discussed previously. However, an NVRAM is physically very different from those devices. Logically an NVRAM is just an SRAM with a battery backup. When the power is turned on, the NVRAM operates just like any other SRAM. When the power is turned off, the NVRAM draws just enough power from the battery to retain its data. NVRAM is fairly common in embedded systems. However, it is expensive than SRAM, because of the battery so its applications are typically limited to the storage of a few hundred bytes of system critical information that cannot be stored in any better way.*1 = Only once using device programmer*

Table 3-1 summarizes the features of each type of memory discussed in this section.

Type	Volatile	Writable	Erase Size	Max Erase Cycles	Cost(per Byte)	Speed
SRAM	Yes	Yes	Byte	Unlimited	Expensive	Fast
DRAM	Yes	Yes	Byte	Unlimited	Moderate	Moderate
Masked ROM	No	No	N/A	N/A	Inexpensive	Fast
PROM	No	No[1]	N/A	N/A	Moderate	Fast
EPROM	No	No[1]	Complete Memory	Limited	Moderate	Fast
EEPROM	No	Yes	Byte	Limited	Expensive	Fast Read, Slow Write/Erase
Flash	No	Yes	Sector	Limited	Moderate	Fast Read, Slow Write/Erase
NVRAM	No	Yes	Byte	Unlimited	Expensive	Fast

1 = Only once using device programmer

Table 3-1: Embedded Memory Classification

NOTE: *Different memory types serve different purposes with each memory type having its strengths and weaknesses, Side-by-side comparison is not always effective.*

3.5 Memory Architecture

Let's consider the architecture and operation of memory chips. The architecture described in this section is applicable to both SRAM and DRAM based designs. At the core of this architecture is a two-dimensional array of bits where each bit may be implemented as an SRAM or DRAM cell. A single bit in this array can be selected or addressed by providing the row and column index of the location of the cell. This bit value stored in the cell can be read into a buffer from which it can be read off-chip. Following shows an example with the related sequence of steps with reference to Figure 3-2.

Let's consider a 1Mbit memory. To access any cell in this memory we must be able to identify each cell. The simplest approach would be to number all of the cells and provide an integer value or number of the cell one wish to access for read or write. That becomes the memory address of the cell and providing this number is referred to as the process of addressing a cell.

How many bits do we need to address 1 Bits? We have $2^{20} = 1M$ and therefore we need a 20 bit number which is referred to as the address of the cell.

However these memory cells (that store the individual bits) are not stored in a linear array that can be addressed in such a simple manner. The single bit cells are arranged in a two-dimensional array of 1024x1024 cells. All of the cells in a row share the same word line or select signal. Thus when a word line is asserted all of the cells in the row will drive their bit values onto the bit lines. Similarly all of the cells in a column share the same bit line. Therefore at any given time only one cell in a column place a value on this shared bit line. Addressing a row or column now only requires 10 bits (2^{10} = 1024). While strictly speaking a cell holds a bit value we will use the term bit and cell interchangeably in this chapter.

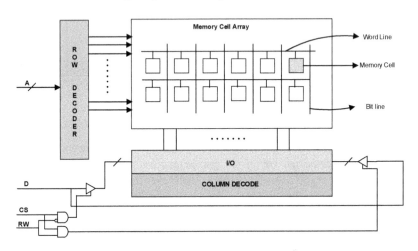

Figure 3-2: Typical organization of Memory Cell in a Memory Array

For the same scenario when a 20 bit address is provided we may see the following sequence of events. The most significant 10 bits of the address are used as a row address to a 10 bit row decoder. Each of the 1024 outputs of the row decoder are connected to one of the 1024 word lines in the array. The selected row will drive their bit values onto the corresponding 1024 bit lines. The 1024 bit values are latched into a row buffer that can be graphically thought of as residing at the bottom of the array in Figure 3-2. The 10-bit column address is used to select one of the 1024 bits from this row buffer and provide the value to the chip output. The access of data from the chip is controlled by two signals. The first is the chip select (CS) which enables the Memory device. The second is a signal that controls whether data is being written to the array (RW=0) or whether data is being read from the array (RW=1). The combination of CS and RW control the tristate devices on the data signals D. The organization shown in Figure 3-2 uses bidirectional signals for data into and out of the memory device rather than having separate input data signals and output data signals.

Consider having four identical memory planes shown in Figure 3-2. Each plane operating concurrently on the same 20 bit address. The result is 4 bits for every access to provide 4Mbits Memory device.

Such a memory would be described as a 1Mx4 memory device since this includes 2^{20} addresses with each address the memory device delivers 4 bits. Other alternative memory data organization for 1Mbit can be 256Kx4, 1Mx1 and 128Kx8. While the total number of bits within the memory device may remain the same, key distinguishing feature is the number of distinct addresses that are supported and the number of bits stored at each address. With a fixed number of total bits on the memory device, the number of distinct addresses provided by the memory device determines the number of bits at each address.

3.6 Building a Memory System

A memory system design will aggregate several memory devices and combinational components. The design is determined by the types of memory devices available, for example 1Mx4 or 4Mx1, and the number of distinct addresses that are to be provided. Solutions are illustrated through the following examples.

Example 1:

Consider a 1Mx8 memory system design using 1Mx4 memory devices. The total number of bits to be provided by the memory system are 8M bits. Each available 1Mx4 memory device provides 4M bits and thus the memory system requires need two memory devices, each providing 4 bits at each address.

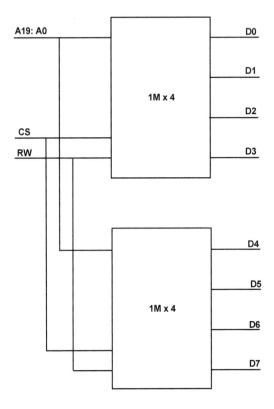

Figure 3-3: Example 1: A 1Mx8 Memory System

One memory device provides the least significant 4-bits at each address and the second chip provides the most significant 4-bits at the same address. The 20-bit address, chip select and Read/Write control goes to both the memory devices.

Example 2:

Consider the same example but for memory system with 2M addresses with a four bits output at each address using the same 1Mx4 memory devices.

The total number of bits in the memory system still remain 8Mbits as in the Example 1. As shown in Figure 3-4 memory system is organized such that each memory device provides 4-bit data and 1M addresses.

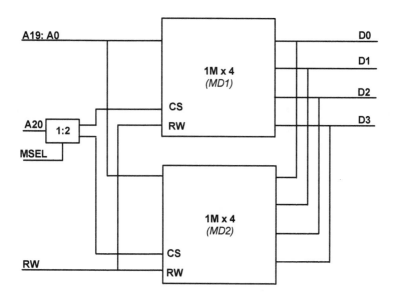

Figure 3-4: Example 2: A 2Mx4 Memory System

Memory device MD1 services the first 1M addresses from 0 to 2^{20} -1. The second memory device MD2 provides the data at the remaining addresses that is addresses from 2^{20} to 2^{21}-1. However this arrangement requires additional control to ensure only one of the two memory devices must be enabled depending on the value of the address. This can be achieved by using the most significant bit of the address as a 1:2 decoder. The most significant bit of an address determines which of the two halves of the address range is being accessed. The outputs of the decoder are connected to the individual memory chip select signals to enable the corresponding memory device. The remaining address lines and the read/write control signal are connected to the corresponding inputs of each memory device. Note that each memory device is provided with same number of address bits, 20 in this case. The memory select signal *MSEL* is used as an enable to the memory system.

This approach represents a common theme. Memory devices are first organized to determine how addresses will be serviced. Some bits of the address as necessary will be used to determine which set of memory devices will deliver data at a specific address. These bits of the address are decoded to enable to correct set of memory devices.

Example 3:

Let's consider the same example but with a memory system with 4M addresses and four bits output at each address for a total of 16Mbits. As in the previous example, building memory system with 1Mx4 memory device will require four memory devices.

Similar to previous example, most straightforward design is one wherein each memory device serves exactly one fourth of the addresses. The first device MA1 will service addresses in the range 0 to 2^{20}-1. The second memory device MA2 will serve addresses in the range 2^{20} to 2^{21}-1 and so on making total address range from 0 to 2^{22}-1.

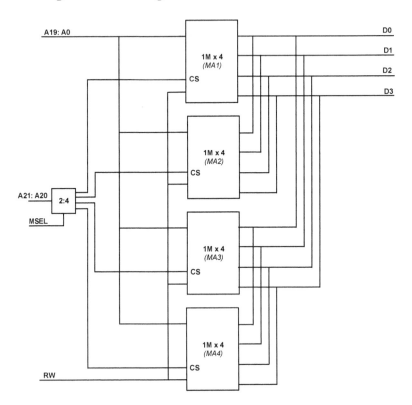

Figure 3-5: Example 3: A 4Mx4 Memory System

The two most significant bits of the address can be used to select one of the memory device. The remaining 20 bits of address are provided to each memory device along with the common read/write control. A 2:4 decoder operating on the two most significant bits of the address is used to select the memory device. As in the previous example *MSEL* is used as a memory system enable signal for the decoder which in turn generates the chip select signals. The memory organization is shown in Figure 3-5. Note that only one memory device is active at a time, however we may have memory organization where this is not necessarily the case as in next example.

Example 4:

Now let's extend the previous example to build a memory system that can provide 2M addresses with 8 bits at each address. Using the same 1Mx4 memory devices, one would need at least two memory devices to provide an 8 bit output at any given address with a total of four memory devices to provide necessary total of 16 Mbits (2M addresses). The memory devices are organized in pairs as shown in Figure 3-6.

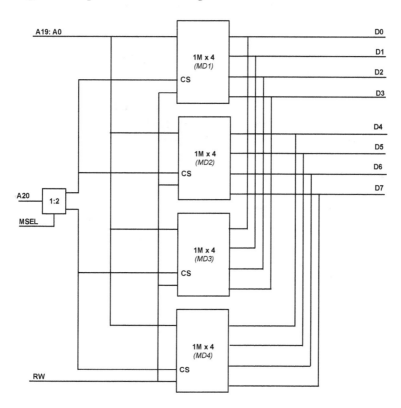

Figure 3-6: Example 4: A 2Mx8 Memory System

The first two memory devices (*MD1* and *MD2*) provide four bits each for the first 1M addresses. The second pair of memory devices (*MD3* and

MD4) does so similarly for the second 1M addresses. A decoder uses the most significant bit of the address to determine which of the two pairs of memory devices will be selected for any specific address.

The preceding examples have illustrated several common ways for constructing memory systems of a given word width using memory devices that provide multibit quantities.

3.7 Programmer's View of Memory

A user or programmer may be only interested in having available a sequence of memory addresses to allow reads or writes to the memory without caring how this particular sequence of addresses are realized, that is, what memory devices are used and how address bits are decoded. Logical view of memory is what programmers and compilers really care about while a physical implementation is the realm of the memory systems designer. This section describes a logical or programmer's view of memory.

A memory device or system can be viewed as a sequence of addresses with a value stored in each address or location. Each memory address can store 8, 16 or 32 bit values. A memory system designed to store 8-bit numbers at each address is referred to as byte addressed memory. Similarly one that is designed to return a 32-bit word from each address is referred as word addressed memory. Although modern microprocessors are 64-bit machines and word addressed memory implies accessing 64-bit quantities.

However, it is quite common for microprocessor systems to provide byte addressed memory even though the word size may be 32 or 64 bits. Therefore we will consistently use a byte addressed memory in our examples which can be viewed as shown in Figure 3-7.

Memory Contents	Memory Address
0x00	0x10010000
0x11	0x10010001
0x22	0x10010002
0x33	0x10010003
0x44	0x10010004
0x55	0x10010005
0x66	0x10010006
0x77	0x10010007
0x88	0x10010008
0x99	0x10010009
0xAA	0x1001000a

Figure 3-7: Logical View of Byte Addressable Memory

The contents of each memory location in the figure is an 8-bit value that shown in hexadecimal notation. The address of each memory location is shown adjacent to the location. Addresses are assumed to be 32-bit values and are also shown in hexadecimal notation. This is just one example of how data could be organized, there could be other models that return 16, 32 or 64 bits rather than 8 bits.

There are good reasons for memory to be most commonly addressed in bytes. Images are organized as arrays of pixels which in black and white images can often be stored as 8-bit values. The ASCII code uses an 8-bit code and storage of character strings typically uses a sequence of byte locations. However the majority of modern high performance processors internally operate on 32 and 64 bits thus storing and retrieving data in 32 and 64 bit quantities.

Let's look at the issues if microprocessor performs accesses to 32-bit words on a byte addressed memory.

The first issue is how are these words stored? For example, consider the need to store the 32-bit quantity 0x00112233 at address 0x10010000. The address refers to a single byte in memory however we wish to store 4 bytes at this location. The straightforward solution is to use the 4 bytes starting at address 0x10010000. After storage the memory will appear as shown in Figure 3-8.

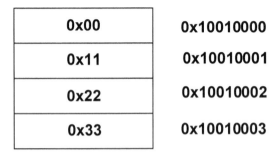

0x00	**0x10010000**
0x11	**0x10010001**
0x22	**0x10010002**
0x33	**0x10010003**

Figure 3-8: Storage of 32-bit words in byte addressable memory

The most significant byte of the word is stored at memory location 0x10010000 and the least significant byte of the word is stored at memory location 0x10010003. This type of storage convention is referred to as "*big endian*" since the *big end* or most significant byte of the word is stored first. This could also have been stored the bytes of the word in memory in the reverse order, that is, the contents of memory location 0x10010000 would have been 0x33 which is the least significant byte or *little end* of the word, likewise this storage convention is referred to as little endian. Different microprocessor vendors will adopt one convention or the other in the way in which words are stored. For example, Intel x86 architectures are little endian while Sun and Apple architectures are big endian. This places a bit of a burden on communication software that transfers data between machines that use different storage conventions since the order of bytes with each word must be reversed.

In general, unless stated otherwise little endian storage convention will be used in this chapter.

If the word size is 32 bits, in a byte addressed memory every fourth address will be the start of a new word. Such addresses are referred to word boundaries. Alternatively if the word size is 64 bits each word will include 8 bytes. Therefore every eighth byte will correspond to a word boundary. In general one can think of 2^k byte boundaries where $0 \leq k \leq n$ and n is the number of bits in the address.

3.8 Memory Hierarchy

Memory is essential component to the operation of an embedded system including the concept of memory hierarchy. While the flat memory system build of a single technology is attractive for its simplicity, a well implemented hierarchy allows a memory system to approach simultaneously the performance of the fastest component, cost per bit of the cheapest component and the energy consumption of most energy-efficient component. The use of a hierarchy allows designers to treat system design as a modularized process, to treat the memory system as an abstraction and to optimize individual subsystems (caches, RAM, DRAMs etc.).

As hierarchies and their components grow more complex, systemic behaviors arising from the complex interaction of the memory system's parts—have begun to dominate. The real loss of performance is not seen in the CPU or caches or DRAM devices but in the subtle interactions between these subsystems and in the manner in which these subsystems are connected. Consequently, it is becoming increasingly important to attempt system level optimization by designing/optimizing each of the parts in isolation. It has now become the case that a memory-systems designer, wishing to build a properly behaved memory hierarchy, must be familiar with issues involved at all levels of an implementation, from cache to DRAM.

A memory hierarchy is designed to provide multiple functions that are seemingly mutually exclusive. Most of the microprocessors and embedded systems expect to operate from a random-access memory (RAM). This is fundamental to the structure of modern embedded software, built upon the von Neumann model in which code and data are essentially the same and reside in the same place (i.e., memory). All requests, whether for instructions or data, go to the random-access memory. At any given moment, any particular datum in memory may be needed; there is no requirement that data reside next to the code that manipulates it, and there is no requirement that two instructions executed one after the other need to be adjacent in memory. Thus, the memory system must be able to handle randomly addressed requests in a manner that favors no particular request. Moreover, this memory must be fast and should match the processor processing speed; otherwise will significantly affect performance.

In a hierarchal memory architecture larger and smaller memories are used to supplement smaller and faster ones. If we put aside the set of CPU registers (as the first level for storing and retrieving information inside the CPU), then a typical memory hierarchy starts with a small, expensive, and relatively fast unit, called the cache. The cache is followed in the hierarchy by a larger, less expensive, and relatively slow main memory unit. Cache and main memory are part of System-on-Chip (SoC). They are followed in the hierarchy by a far larger, less expensive, and much slower external memories typically NOR/NAND Flash. The objective behind designing a memory hierarchy is to have a memory system that performs as if it consists entirely of the fastest unit and with the cost dominated by the cost of the slowest unit.

The memory hierarchy can be characterized by a number of parameters. Among these parameters are the *access type*, *capacity*, *cycle time*, *latency*, *bandwidth*, and *cost*. The term *access* refers to the action that physically takes place during a read or write operation. The *capacity* of a memory level is usually measured in bytes. The *cycle time* is defined as the time elapsed from the start of a read operation to the start of a subsequent read. The *latency* is defined as the time interval between the request for information and the access of the first bit of that information. The *bandwidth* provides a measure of the number of bits per second that can be accessed. The *cost* of a memory level is usually provided as *Dollars per megabytes*. Figure 3-9 depicts a typical memory hierarchy.02

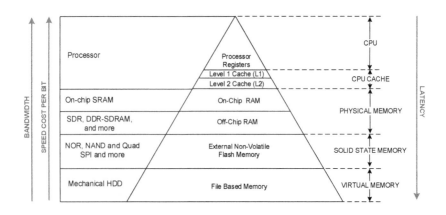

Figure 3-9: Typical Memory Hierarchy for an embedded device

Table 3-2: Typical values of Memory Hierarchy Parameters provides typical values of the memory hierarchy parameters. The term random access refers to the fact that any access to any memory location takes the same fixed amount of time regardless of the actual memory location and/or the sequence of accesses that take place. For example, if a write operation to memory location 100 takes 15 ns and if this read is followed by a write operation to memory location 3000, then the write operation will take 15 ns. This is to be compared to sequential access in which if access to location 100 takes 15 ns, and if a consecutive access to location 101 takes 20 ns, then it is expected that an access to location 300 may take 1000 ns. This is because the memory has to cycle through locations 100 to 300, with each location requiring 5 ns.

	Access type	Capacity	Latency	Bandwidth	Cost/ MB
CPU Registers	Random	64-1024Bytes	1-10ns	System Clock rate	High
Cache Memory	Random	8-512KB	15-20ns	Slightly lower system clock rate	$500
Main Memory(on-chip)	Random	32-512KB	20-70ns	100-200MB/s	$20-$50
Main Memory(off-chip)	Random	Up-to 512MB	50-70ns	Up-to 1600MB/sec	$20-$50/GB
Disk(HDD) Memory	Direct	Up-to 8TB	2.9-12ms	140 MB/s	$0.10/GB2
SSD(Nand)	Random	120 to 512GB	0.1 ms	100-600 MB/s	$0.37/GB1

1, 2: Based on Wikipedia, dated Feb-2015

Table 3-2: Typical values of Memory Hierarchy Parameters

NOTE: *Data in the table above should only be taken as relative comparison. Numbers may not be accurate during the time book would be released. Also note that numbers in context to bandwidth are de-rated as to what are applicable to embedded system instead of max that can be achieved on modern computers or servers.*

The efficiency of a memory hierarchy depends on the principle of moving information into the fast memory infrequently and accessing it many times before replacing it with new information. This principle is possible due to a well-known phenomenon called *"locality of reference"* [15], i.e. within a given period of time, programs tend to reference relatively confined area of memory repeatedly. There exists two forms of locality. *"Spatial locality"* [15] refers to the phenomenon that when a given address has been referenced, it is most likely that addresses near it will be referenced within a short period of time, e.g. consecutive instruction in a straight-line program. *"Temporal locality"* [15], on the other hand, refers to the phenomenon that once a particular memory item has been referenced, it is most likely that it will be referenced again within a short period of time, e.g. an instruction in a program loop.

3.9 Memory Map

There are two basic types of architecture: Harvard and Von Neumann. Microcontrollers most often use a Harvard or a modified Harvard-based architecture.

3.9.1 Von Neumann Architecture

Von Neumann architecture has a single, common memory space where both program instructions and data are stored. There is a single data bus which fetches both instructions and data. Each time the CPU fetches a program instruction it may have to perform one or more read/write operations to data memory space. It must wait until these subsequent operations are complete before it can fetch and decode the next program instruction. The advantage to this architecture lies in its simplicity and economy.

NOTE: *On some Von Neumann machines the program can read from and write to CPU registers, including the program counter. This can be dangerous as you can point the PC at memory blocks outside program memory space. Careless PC manipulation can cause errors which require a hard reset* [15].

A memory map is a diagram which shows how the microcontroller memory is used. The following example map is from the Motorola MC68HC705C8 microcontroller configured for 176 bytes of RAM and 7744 bytes of PROM [15]:

Contents	Address
I/O 32 bytes	0x0000
	0x001F
User Prom 48 bytes	0x0020
	0x004F
176 Bytes of RAM	0x0050
	0x00BF
STACK	0x00C0
	0x00FF
User PROM 96 bytes	0x0100
	0x015F
User PROM 7584 bytes	0x0160
	0x1EFF
Boot ROM 223 bytes	0x1F00
	0x1FDE
Option Register	0x1FDF
Boot ROM vectors 16 bytes	0x1FE0
	0x1FEF
Unused 4 bytes	0x1FF3
User PROM vectors 12 bytes	0x1FF4
	0x1FFF

Figure 3-10: Von Neumann Memory Map for the MC68705C8 [15]

3.9.2 Harvard Architecture

Harvard architecture computers have separate memory areas for program instructions and data. There are two or more internal data buses which allow simultaneous access to both instructions and data. The CPU fetches instructions on the program memory bus. If the fetched instruction requires an operation on data memory, the CPU can fetch the next program instruction while it uses the data bus for its data operation. This speeds up execution time at the cost of more hardware complexity. Since Harvard machines assume that only instructions are stored in program memory space, one problem would be how to write and access data stored in program memory space? For example, a data value declared as a C constant must be stored in ROM as a constant value. Different microcontrollers have different solutions to this problem. A good C compiler automatically generates the code to suit the target hardware's requirements. Some chips have special instructions allowing the retrieval of information from program memory space. These instructions are always more complex or expensive than the equivalent instructions for fetching data from data memory.

Typically these chips have a register analogous to the program counter (PC) which refers to addresses in program space. Also, some chips support the use of any 16 bit value contained in data space as a pointer into the program address space. These chips have special instructions to use these data pointers.

NOTE: *It is important to understand how Harvard architecture part deals with data in program space. It is possible to generate more efficient code using symbolic constants declared with #define directives instead of declared constants. You may also create global variables for constant values.*

The following memory map is from the Microchip PIC16C74. Notice that program memory is paged and data memory is banked. The stack is implemented in hardware and the developer has no access to it [15].

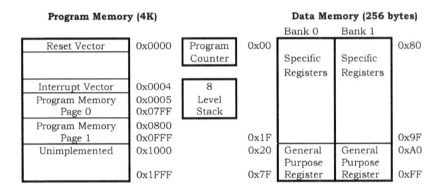

Figure 3-11: Harvard Memory Map PIC16C74 [15]

3.10 Handling Endianness

Endianness describes how multi-byte data is represented by an embedded system.

Consider the analogy of communicating the word ""TEST" using four packets of one character each. The transmitting party sends data in following order: "T" (transmitted first) → "E" → "S" → "T" (transmitted last). Without sufficient information, the receiving party can capture and assemble the data in 16 different combinations. Similarly incase the word is communicated using two packets of two character each ("TE" and "ST"), receiving party can assemble data either as "TEST" or "STTE", latter being incorrect. For similar reasons, the difference in Endian-architecture is an issue when software or data is shared between systems unless all embedded systems are designed with same Endian-architecture. Incase software accesses all the data as 32-bit words; the issue of endianness is not relevant. However, if the software executes instructions that operate on 8 or 16 bits data at a time, and the data need to be mapped at specific memory addresses (such as with memory-mapped I/O), then the issue of endianness will have to dealt with.

3.10.1 Definition

Endianness defines the format how multi-byte data is stored in embedded memory. It describes the location of the most significant byte (MSB) and least significant byte (LSB) of an address in memory. This does not really matter for a true 32-bit system where data is always stored as 32 bit in the system memory, however for a system that maps bytes or 16 bit half words to 32-bit words in the system memory, endianness mismatch can result in data integrity.

There are two type of Endianness-architecture, Big-Endian (BE) and Little-Endian (LE). Big-Endian stores the MSB at the lowest memory address. Little-Endian stores the LSB at the lowest memory address. The lowest memory address of multi-byte data is considered the starting address of the data. Table 3-3 shows Big Endian and Little Endian representation of a 32 bit hex value 0xAABBCCDD that gets stored in memory. *Byte 0* represents the lowest memory address.

Endian Architecture	Byte 0	Byte 1	Byte 2	Byte 3
Big Endian	AA (MSB)	BB	CC	DD (LSB)
Little Endian	DD (LSB)	CC	BB	AA (MSB)

Table 3-3: Big Endian and Little Endian Byte Ordering

Note that stored multi-byte data field is the same for both types of Endianness as long as the data is referenced in its native data type i.e. 32 bit. However, when the data is accessed as bytes or half-words, the order of the sub-fields depends on the endian configuration of the system. If a program stores the above value at location 0x100 as a word and then fetches the data as individual bytes, two possible orders exist.

In the case of a little-endian system, the data bytes will have the order depicted in Table 3-4.

Address	Data
0x0100	DD
0x0101	CC
0x0102	BB
0x0103	AA

Table 3-4: Little Endian Addressing

Note that the rightmost byte of the word is the first byte in the memory location at 0x100. This is why this format is called little-endian; the least significant byte of the word occupies the lowest byte address within the word in memory.

If the program executes in a big-endian system, the word has the byte order in memory shown in Table 3-5.

Address	Data
0x0100	AA
0x0101	BB
0x0102	CC
0x0103	DD

Table 3-5: Big Endian Addressing

The least significant byte of the word is stored in the high order byte address. The most significant byte of the word occupies the low order byte address, which is why this format is called big-endian.

When dealing with half-words, the memory address must be a multiple of two. Thus the value in Table 3-3 will occupy two half-word addresses: 0x100 and 0x102. Table 3-6 shows the layout for both endian configurations.

Address	Little Endian	Big Endian
0x0100	CCDD	AABB
0x0102	AABB	CCDD

Table 3-6: Half Word Endian Order

Note: *Within the half-word, the bytes maintain the same order as they have in the word format. In little-endian mode, the least significant half-word resides at the low-order* address (0x100) and the most significant half-word resides at the high-order address (0x102). For the big-endian case, the layout is reversed.

Generally the issue of endianness is transparent to both programmers and users. However, the issue becomes trivial when data must cross between endian formats.

3.10.2 Little-Endian versus Big-Endian

One may see a lot of discussion about the relative merits of the two formats, mostly religious arguments based on the relative merits of the PC versus the Mac; however both formats have their advantages and disadvantages.

In *Little Endian* form, since lowest order byte is at offset "0" and is accessed first, assembly language instructions for accessing 1, 2, 4, or longer byte number proceed in exactly the same way for all formats. Also, because of the 1:1 relationship between address offset and byte number (offset 0 is byte 0), multiple precision math routines are correspondingly easy to write.

In *Big Endian* form, since the higher-order byte come first, it is easy to test whether the number is positive or negative by looking at the byte at offset zero. Thus there is no need to receive the complete packet of bytes to know the sign information. The numbers are also stored in the order in which they are printed out, so binary to decimal routines are particularly efficient.

Let's look at hex value of 0x12345678 stored in different endian formats within the memory.

Address	00	01	02	03
Big-endian	12	34	56	78
Little-endian	78	56	34	12

One would notice that reading a hex dump is certainly easier in a big-endian machine since numbers are normally read from left to right (lower to higher address).

Most bitmapped graphics (displays and memory arrangements) are mapped with a *MSB on the left* scheme which means that shifts and stores of graphical elements larger than a byte are handled naturally by the architecture. This is a major performance disadvantage for little-endian machines since one have to keep reversing the byte order when working with large graphical elements.

Table 3-7 lists several popular computer systems and their Endian Architectures. Note that some CPUs can be either big or little endian (Bi-Endian) by setting a processor register to the desired endian-architecture.

Processor	Endian Architecture
ARM	Bi-Endian
IBM Power PC	Bi-Endian
Intel® 80x86	Little-Endian
Intel® Itanium® processor family	Bi-Endian
Motorola 68K	Big-Endian

Table 3-7: Computer System Endianness

Most embedded communication processors and custom solutions associated with the data plane are Big-Endian (i.e. PowerPC, SPARC, etc.). Because of this, legacy code on these processors is often written specifically for network byte order (Big-Endian).

Some of the common file formats and their endian order are listed in Table 3-8:

File Format	Endian Format
Adobe Photoshop	Big Endian
BMP (Windows and OS/2 Bitmaps)	Little Endian
GIF	Little Endian
JPEG	Big Endian
PCX (PC Paintbrush)	Little Endian
QTM (Quicktime Movies)	Little Endian
Microsoft RIFF (.WAV & .AVI)	Bi-Endian
Microsoft RTF (Rich Text Format)	Little Endian
SGI (Silicon Graphics)	Big Endian
TIFF	Bi-Endian
XWD (X Window Dump)	Bi-Endian

Table 3-8: Common File Formats and their Endian Order

What this means is that any time numbers are written to a file, one needs to know how file is supposed to be constructed, for example if graphics file (such as a .BMP file) is written on a *Big Endian* machine , byte order first needs to be reversed else *standard* program to read the file won't work.

The Windows .BMP format, since it was developed on *Little Endian* architecture, insists on the *Little Endian* format regardless of the platform being used.

Also note that some CPUs can be either big or little endian (Bi-Endian) by setting a processor register to the desired endian-architecture.

3.10.3 Issues dealing with Endianness Mismatch

Endianness doesn't matter on a single system. It matters only when two systems are trying to communicate. Every processor and every communication protocol must choose one type of endianness or the other. Thus, two processors with different endianness will conflict if they communicate through a memory device. Similarly, a little-endian processor trying to communicate over a big-endian network will need to do software-byte reordering.

An endianness difference can cause problems if an embedded system unknowingly tries to read binary data written in the opposite format from a shared memory location or file.

Another area where endianness is an issue is in network communications. Since different processor types (big-endian and little-endian) can be on the same network, they must be able to communicate with each other. Therefore, network stacks and communication protocols must also define their endianness. Otherwise, two nodes of different endianness would be unable to communicate. This is a more substantial example of endianness affecting the embedded programmer.

As it turns out, all of the protocol layers in the TCP/IP suite are defined as big-endian. In other words, any 16- or 32-bit value within the various layer headers (for example, an IP address, a packet length, or a checksum) must be sent and received with its most significant byte first.

Let's say you wish to establish a TCP socket connection to a computer whose IP address is 192.0.1.7. IPv4 uses a unique 32-bit integer to identify each network host. The dotted decimal IP address must be translated into such an integer.

The multibyte integer representation used by the TCP/IP protocols is sometimes called *network byte order*. Even if the computers at each end are little-endian, multibyte integers passed between them must be converted to network byte order prior to transmission across the network, and then converted back to little-endian at the receiving end.

Suppose an 80x86-based, little-endian PC is talking to a SPARC-based, big-endian server over the Internet. Without further manipulation, the 8086 processor would convert 192.0.1.7 to the little-endian integer 0x070100C0 and transmit the bytes in the following order: 0x07, 0x01, 0x00, 0xC0. The SPARC would receive the bytes in the following order: 0x07, 0x01, 0x00, 0xC0. The SPARC would reconstruct the bytes into a big-endian integer 0x070100c0, and misinterpret the address as 7.1.0.192. [10].

Preventing this sort of confusion leads to an annoying little implementation detail for TCP/IP stack developers. If the stack will run on a little-endian processor, it will have to reorder (at runtime) the bytes of every multibyte data field within the various layers' headers. If the stack will run on a big-endian processor, there's nothing to worry about. For the stack to be portable (that is, to be able to run on processors of both types), it will have to decide whether or not to do this reordering. The decision is typically made at compile time.

Another good example is Flash programming for a device. Most common flash memories are 8 or 16 bit wide. Most of the 32 bit Flash memory interfaces that exist would actually require two interleaved 16-bit devices. Programming operations on these devices involve 8- or 16-bit data write operations at specific addresses within each device. For this reason, the software engineer must know and understand the endian configuration of the hardware in order to successfully program the flash device(s).

Code which will be executed directly from an 8- or 16-bit flash device must be stored in a way that instructions will be properly recognized when they are fetched by the processor. This may be affected by the endian configuration of the system. Compilers typically have a switch that can be used to control the endianness of the code image that will be programmed into the flash device.

3.10.4 Accessing 32-bit Memory

The following example shows 8-bit, 16-bit, and 32-bit accesses to a 32-bit memory.

The relationship of a byte address to specific bits on the 32-bit data bus is shown in the Table 3-9.

Address [1:0]	Big Endian(BE)	Little Endian(LE)
"00"	Data [31:24]	Data [7:0]
"01"	Data [23:16]	Data [15:8]
"10"	Data [15:8]	Data [23:16]
"11"	Data [7:0]	Data [31:24]

Table 3-9: Address-Data mapping for different Endian Systems

Table 3-10 shows the data byte mapping for little and big endian system with 8-bit, 16-bit and 32-bit access.

	Data[31:24]	Data[23:16]	Data[15:8]	Data[7:0]
Data[31:0]	0A	0B	0C	0D
Byte Address(BE)	0	1	2	3
Byte Address(LE)	3	2	1	0
32-bit Read				
32-bit read at Address "00" (BE)	0A	0B	0C	0D
32-bit read at Address "00" (LE)	0A	0B	0C	0D
16-bit Read				
16-bit read at Address "00" (BE)	0A	0B	--	--
16-bit read at Address "00" (LE)	--	--	0C	0D
16-bit read at Address "10" (BE)	--	--	0C	0D
16-bit read at Address "10" (LE)	0A	0B	--	--
8-bit Read				
8-bit read at Address "00" (BE)	0A	--	--	--
8-bit read at Address "00" (LE)	--	--	--	0D

8-bit read at Address "01" (BE)	--	0B	--	--
8-bit read at Address "01" (LE)	--	--	0C	--
8-bit read at Address "10" (BE)	--	--	0C	--
8-bit read at Address "10" (LE)	--	0B	--	--
8-bit read at Address "11" (BE)	--	--	--	0D
8-bit read at Address "11" (LE)	0A	--	--	--

Table 3-10: Address-Data mapping for different Endian system with 8, 16 and 32 bit access size

3.10.5 Dealing with Endianness Mismatch

Endianness mismatch is bound to happen in System-On-Chip (SoC) that includes several IPs few being sourced from 3rd party company that may not support same Endianness type as the processor. One of the easiest ways to deal with Endianness mismatch is to choose one *Endianness type (i.e. Little-Endian or Big-Endian)* for the system and convert all other modules with different Endianness to the target *Endianness type*.

Typically Endianness is dictated by the CPU architecture implementation of the system, so it is highly recommended that target *Endianness type* should match with processor Endianness. Another consideration while sourcing 3rd party IPs should be to check if IP support *Bi-Endian* architecture such that system integrator could easily program the IP to work as *Big-Endian* or *Little Endian* for a seamless integration with the system. For the cases that do not satisfy these requirements, one of the techniques mentioned in the section must be used to resolve Endianness conflict. In case there is no programmable option, the endianness mismatch can be removed during integrating of the IP in the SoC.

There are two ways to interface opposite-endianness peripherals. Depending on the application requirements, either the address can be chosen to remain constant (i.e. Address Invariance where bytes remain at same address) or bit ordering can be chosen to remain constant (Data Invariance where addresses are changed).

3.10.6 Preserve Data Integrity (Data Invariance)

When a core or IP within a SoC operates on a single or multi byte field, the MSB is on the left hand side of the field and the LSB is on the right hand side of the field. That is, if a 16 bit field holds an integer and the desired operation is to increment it, a "1" is added to the LSB and any needed carries are propagated from the LSB (on the right) towards the MSB (on the left). This operation is the same for either big or little endian address architectures.

This leads to one of the main issues in mixing cores and other IPs of different endian address architectures since a multi-byte field has different byte address based on the endian mode, if a multi-byte field is be manipulated as a single entry, bit ordering within the entry must be preserved as it is moved across various IPs.

This same issue applies to multi-bit fields that cross byte boundaries. Consider an IP that has a 16 bit control register in its programming model. If the bit field [8:7] within this control register defines a control field, then it is required that the relationship of these 16 bits remain constant for all accesses to the control register.

In order to understand the process to match endianness keeping the data bit order inact, consider a serial frame that is received by a little endian peripheral and the data is then stored by the DMA/CPU into memory location while the CPU/DMA is big endian. The serial frame is received as header first followed by rest of the frame. See Figure 3-12.

The serial frame received is stored in the peripheral's memory in the order *Type*, *H2*, *H1*, and *H0*, which is little endian. It is possible that fields in the frame can span over multiple bytes and not end on a byte boundary (Figure 3-13). For example, the status field can be of 12 bits. Hence it is important for the application that this data is not changed due to endianness conversion as the software would process the data in that order.

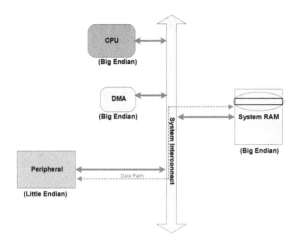

Figure 3-12: Data flow from Little-Endian Peripheral to System Memory (Address Variance)

In Figure 3-12, the data is stored in peripheral's memory using little endian addressing. Now when this data is transferred to the system RAM, which is big endian, it should be ensured that the bit ordering of the data is not changed. In order to achieve this in hardware, the address that is used to access the peripheral RAM's memory is modified. The modification of address is done based on the size of transfer, as shown in table Table 3-11:

Size of Transfer	Little Endian Address	Mapped Big Endian Address
8-bits	0x0003	0x0000
	0x0002	0x0001
	0x0001	0x0002
	0x0000	0x0003
16-bits	0x0002	0x0000
	0x0000	0x0002
32-bits	0x0000	0x0000

Table 3-11: Address Variance for Endianness Matching

Using the above logic, the last two LSBs of the address bus is inverted and the data bus is used as is.

With the above scheme the endianness conversion is transparent to the software and it is ensured that data integrity is not compromised during after endianness conversion.

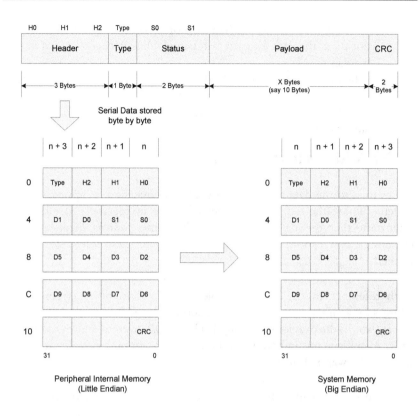

Figure 3-13: Interfacing Little Endian Memory to Big Endian Memory using Data Invariance

Data Flow:

Data flow from a little endian peripheral to big endian memory using data invariance is described below:

1. DMA generates byte read access to peripheral's memory.
2. Let's take an example where the address generated by system is 0x00. With the data variance implementation, the address seen by little endian Peripheral RAM is 0x03.
3. This is decoded by peripheral RAM as access to bits 31:24 or *Type* field as shown in Figure 3-13.
4. Peripheral outputs the data as {"Type", "0x000000"} (32-bit output).
5. DMA generates byte write access to system's big endian memory.
6. The address generated is again 0x00 (byte access).
7. The big endian memory decodes the access as write to bits 31:24.

8. Since data from little endian memory is on the same byte location, the data integrity is retained while data gets stored in big endian RAM.
9. The process continues for other bytes that need to be transferred from peripheral RAM to system RAM.
10. For 16-bit and 32-bit access, the above process is same with address being changed as shown in Table 3-11.

3.10.7 Address Invariance

In contrast to the data invariant endianness conversion, in applications or systems where the data is not expected to be in specific order but it is important that the data bytes be at the same address locations after endianness conversion; the address invariant endianness conversion can be applied.

With reference to the same example of a serial frame reception, for a address invariant system the byte *Type* should always be accessed at address offset 0x3. In the previous section, this byte had different address offset. In order to achieve this in hardware, the data read from the peripheral RAM's memory is swapped or modified.

The address invariant endianness conversion is shown in Figure 3-14.

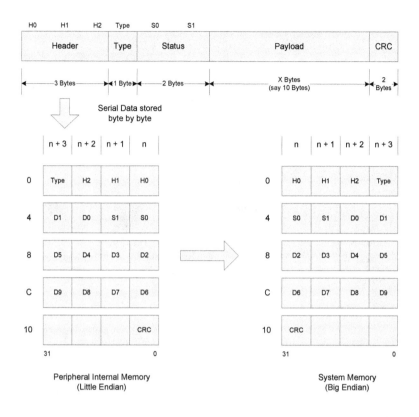

Figure 3-14: Interfacing Little Endian Memory to Big Endian Memory using Address Invariance

Data Flow:

Data flow from a little endian peripheral to big endian memory using address invariance is described below:

1. DMA generates byte read access to peripheral's memory.
2. Let's take an example where the address generated by system is 0x00. Address invariance implementation keeps the address same.
3. This is decoded by peripheral RAM as access to bits 7:0 or "H0" field as shown in Figure 3-14.
4. Peripheral outputs the data as {"0x000000", "H0"} (32-bit output). Due to above address invariance implementation for endianness matching, data to system's RAM is modified to {"H0", "0x000000"}.
5. DMA generates byte write access to system's big endian memory.
6. The address generated is again 0x00 (byte access).

7. The big endian memory decodes the access as write to bits 31:24.
8. Since after endianness conversion, data from little endian memory is on the same address location, the data gets stored in the big endian RAM.
9. The process continues for other bytes that need to be transferred from peripheral RAM to system RAM.
10. For 16-bit and 32-bit access, the above process is same with output data being swapped as shown in Table 3-11

3.10.8 Software Byte Swapping

Swapping byte is an alternate way to achieve endianness conversion. This mode is useful in systems where the endianness is decided by the application itself. Thus, there is no need for a hardware fix to deal with endianness mismatch. The byte swap methods of Endian-neutral code uses byte swap controls to determine whether a byte swap must be performed.

3.10.8.1   Methods

Various byte swap methods that are commonly used in software are:

- Swap assembly instructions
- Software library macros for swapping of bytes
- Protocol specific swap functions
- Customized swap functions

Swap Assembly instructions

Some microcontroller's instruction sets have predefined swap functions which can be used by software to implement application specific endianness conversion.

Swap library macros

Several software programming languages also provide in built macros to implement byte swapping for endianness conversion in an application.

Protocol specific macros

All communication protocols must define the Endianness of the protocol so that there is a predefined agreement on how nodes at opposite ends know how to communicate. Protocols like TCP/IP, defines the network byte order as Big-Endian and the IP Header of a TCP/IP packet contains several multi-byte fields. Computers having Little-Endian architecture must reorder the bytes in the TCP/IP header information into Big-Endian format before transmitting the data and likewise, need to reorder the TCP/IP information received into Little-Endian format.

Limitation

Implementing byte swapping functions in software always adds unwanted overhead. The byte-swapping overhead, though it undeniably exists, can be readily recovered when there is a significant amount of packet processing to be done, especially with the higher frequency processors.

3.11 Bit Banding

Bit Banding is a method of performing atomic bitwise modifications to memory. Usually changing a word in memory requires a read-modify-write cycle (Figure 3-15).

```
Read (0xaa) from A to register
Modify (0xaa to 0xab)
Write (0xab) to A
```

Figure 3-15: Read-Modify-Write Operation

If this operation is interrupted there can be data loss as shown in Figure 3-16 where (0x33) data is lost due to interrupt.

```
Read (0xaa) from A to register
Interrupt!
Write (0x33) to A
Return!
Modify (0xaa to 0xab)
Write (0xab) to A
```

Figure 3-16: Read-Modify-Write operation interrupted

99

This is avoided by disabling interrupts using a supervisor mode or by using bit-banding as shown here.

ARM Cortex-M® core provides capability of bit-banding. Figure 3-17 shows bit-banding mapping in NXP LPC176x/5x User Manual supported by ARM Cortex-M3® core [16].

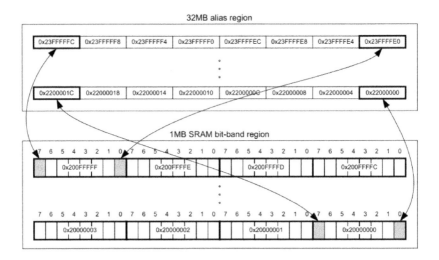

Figure 3-17: Bit-Band Mapping in NXP LPC176x

Two 1MB *bit-band* regions, one in the peripheral memory area and one in the SRAM memory areas are each mapped to a 32MB virtual *alias* region. Each bit in the bit-band region is mapped to a 32bit word in the alias region [16].

The first bit in the *bit-band* peripheral memory is mapped to the first word in the alias region, the second bit to the second word etc.

Writing a value to the alias region with Least Significant Bit i.e. bit [0] set to 1 will write a value of 1 to the bit-band bit. Conversely writing a value of 0 will clear the bit-band bit. The value of the bits [31:1] in the alias region for any word are unmapped and will have no effect on the bit-band value.

One can use this method to do atomic (non interruptible) changes to a bit in SRAM or peripheral mapped memory. If atomic changes are not required, then this process can be slower as change is limited to single bit at a time. In certain circumstances (changing lots of bits) it may be quicker to disable interrupts, make the changes and re-enable interrupts.

4. System Boot

4.1 Introduction

Boot process is the sequence of steps that a system performs when the power is switched on until the application is loaded. Though it sounds simple and obvious that main job of a bootloader is to load the operating system, the process is often complex and understood differently by a hardware as well as software engineer.

This chapter takes deep dive into boot process covering both hardware as well as software aspects of an embedded system. A program cannot be loaded into memory unless a program has already been loaded into memory. This leads to the *"chicken and egg"* situation. The boot process solves this dilemma. This is often a multi-step complex process and involves several sub-steps before a program gets loaded in the system memory.

Microsoft Windows® being common and standard Operating system to what engineers(or even a non-engineering community) are aware about and can relate to, next section describes Windows® XP boot process as an example to start with but later sections are restricted to boot process and options in an embedded application.

Any boot process be it Windows®, Linux® or embedded Real Time Operating System (RTOS) would start when a power is applied to the system and subsequent system reset is removed. There are several things that can happen during Power on Reset (POR) assertion that includes hardware peripherals configuration if values need to be different than default settings and this specifically needs to be done before reset is released so that after reset, chip would have some desired configuration to boot from. There can be various hardware reset configuration schemes that can be made available in an embedded microcontroller. These schemes are discussed in later sections of the chapter.

Over the last two decades boot process has really evolved from simple DOS based boot to more complicated multi-OS or even peripheral boot like USB that allows an image to be booted from a USB device. Later is getting more popular recently in Industrial/embedded applications as it provides lot of flexibility for example during a software corruption where system(or equipment) needs to be loaded with the new firmware, the technique allows service engineer to just copy new software on a USB pen drive and boot the system from the USB drive rather than taking big piece of equipment back to the manufacturer saving thousands of dollars that could just be incurred in transportation of the equipment. To enable this, hardware as well as software capabilities need to be understood that allow an embedded system to boot from various interfaces like USB, PCI-Express, SDHC card apart from standard boot from on-chip or off-chip Memories.

Final section of the chapter covers U-Boot which is an open source firmware and is widely used in embedded platforms. U-Boot is a Linux® based bootloader that can load and starts the OS automatically (auto-boot) or alternatively, it allows users to run commands to start OS and supports booting from variety of interfaces.

4.2 System Boot – Windows® XP

Let's begin with simple x86 boot sequence shown in Figure 4-1 which is self-explanatory [17].

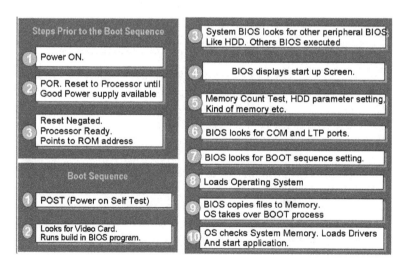

Figure 4-1: Boot Process for Windows® XP

Windows® XP follows the same step but have more sophistication with details shown below with step-wise explanation [17].

1. *Power Supply Switched ON and POR* - Boot starts with Power ON. Processor is kept in reset. When all voltages and current levels are acceptable, the supply indicates that the power is stable and sends the Power Good signal to the processor.

2. *POR Negated:* With the availability of good power supply, reset to the processor is negated so as to allow the CPU to begin operation. CPU points to the ROM address and starts executing the ROM BIOS (one line description on BIOS) code.

3. *Power On Self Test(POST)* : The CPU starts executing the ROM BIOS code. The ROM BIOS performs a basic test (POST) of central hardware to verify basic functionality any errors that occur at this point in the boot process will be reported by means of 'beep-codes' because the video subsystem has not yet been initialized.

4. *Video Card Initialization:* BIOS looks for video card adaptor. Startup BIOS routine scan memory addresses (C000:0000 through C780:0000) to find video ROM. The Video Test initializes the video adapter, tests the video card and video memory, and displays configuration information. Depending on whether this a cold-start or warm-start, ROM BIOS executes a full POST. If this is warm-start, memory test portion of the POST is skipped.

5. *CMOS readout from BIOS*: BIOS locates and reads the configuration information stored in CMOS(small area of memory-usually 64 bytes maintained by small coin cell on the motherboard). CMOS indicates things like Time, boot order etc.

6. *Master Boot Record(MBR):* If the first bootable disk is a fixed disk the BIOS examines the very first sector of the disk for a Master Boot Record (MBR). A Master Boot Record is made up of two parts - the partition table which describes the layout of the fixed disk and the partition loader code which includes instructions for continuing the boot process.

7. *Boot Loader :* The partition loader (or Boot Loader) examines the partition table for a partition marked as active. The partition loader then searches the very first sector of that partition for a Boot Record.

8. *NTLDR :* The active partition's boot record is checked for a valid boot signature and if found the boot sector code is executed as a program. The loading of Windows® XP is controlled by the file

NTLDR which is a hidden, system file that resides in the root directory of the system partition.

9. *NTLDR Initial Phase:* During the initial phase NTLDR switches the processor from real-mode to protected mode which places the processor in 32-bit memory mode and turns memory paging on. It then loads the appropriate mini-file system drivers to allow NTLDR to load files from a partition formatted with any of the files systems (FAT-16, FAT-32 or NTFS) supported by XP.

10. *NTLDR OS Selection:* If the file BOOT.INI is located in the root directory NTLDR will read it's contents into memory. If BOOT.INI contains entries for more than one operating system NTLDR will stop the boot sequence at this point, display a menu of choices, and wait for a specified period of time for the user to make a selection.

11. *Hardware Detection :* NTLDR will continue boot process by locating and loading the DOS based NTDETECT.COM program to perform hardware detection.

12. *Kernel Load :* After selecting a hardware configuration NTLDR begins loading the XP kernel (NTOSKRNL.EXE). During this process, the screen is cleared and a series of white rectangles progress across the bottom of the screen

13. *Load Device Drivers:* NTLDR now loads device drivers that are marked as boot devices. With the loading of these drivers NTLDR relinquishes control of the computer.

14. *Kernel Initialization:* At this point, system displays a graphics screen with a status bar indicating load status ("loading Windows®"). During later phase of initialization, system is prepared to accept interrupts from the devices. Initialization also indicates I/O Manager that begins to load all the system drivers files picking it up where NTLDR left off. Last task for this initialization phase is to launch Session Manager Subsystem (SMSS). SMSS is responsible for creating the user-mode environment.

15. *Windows® XP start-up screen:* SMSS loads the win32k.sys device driver which implements the Win32 graphics subsystem. The XP boot process is not considered complete until a user has successfully logged onto the system. The process is begun by the WINLOGON.EXE file which is loaded as a service by the kernel and displays the logon dialog box.

4.3 Why Boot?

Microcontrollers that do not have a specific boot ROM usually jump to a memory location in an internal memory device, typically Flash and start executing instructions. This internal memory location is generally fixed, and the execution begins when the processor transitions out of the reset sequence.

In these processors, code and data are already programmed into an internal Flash device. The only timing constraints relate to the intervals after power-up sequences to ensure that the flash is ready to be accessed at least as quickly as the processor is ready to make an access.

For the case where there is no internal Flash and system relies on external memory, execution out of the external memory is slower than running code from faster internal memory because the flash memory runs at a clock speed that is typically much lower than the speed at which the processor's core runs.

If the code is simply executed in place ("*XIP*") from flash, enabling instruction cache can significantly increase the speed of execution. This is especially true when burst flash is used, because the synchronous access patterns of these devices are friendly to the typical cache-line fill sizes of embedded processors.

While this method of starting a processor's execution is common, it constrains the code storage options of a system. For example, a NOR flash will cost more than a commensurate serial SPI-based device, but the NOR flash provides faster access than does the serial device.

Because of this, the first code that is executed is often a small code segment that is used to set up the transfers needed to bring the remaining code into internal memory space, where it can then be executed at the core processor frequency.

When the transfers are complete, the processor then jumps to the start of the internal memory space where it executes the application code that was just transferred.

4.4 Demystifying Reset Configuration Schemes

Since Reset is the first sequence that happens prior to any code execution or system boot this section would discuss various reset options and schemes and way it impacts the boot process.

4.4.1 Reset configuration during Boot

Older generation of microcontrollers used to have one fixed state of the entire registers configuration after reset is deasserted. This would mean a fixed value for parameters like clock speed configuration, start address location, pad slew, drive strengths, external memory port size, peripheral enable/disable etc. This would enforce a restriction on the way a chip is used just after reset is deasserted. For example if on-chip oscillator which provides the clock to some on or off chip peripherals is disabled after reset, those peripherals would only be able to work after oscillator is enabled in software program. In some of the simpler systems this behavior should work perfectly fine but may not meet the requirements if same chip is used for several different applications and require different configuration during reset. To provide flexibility to user in order to have desired configuration of some special registers after reset, different reset configuration design schemes can be implemented in a microcontroller. Some of the microcontrollers also support multi-configuration schemes where selection of any particular scheme is done by reading the state of specific pins on the microcontroller during reset.

Four different reset schemes are presented in this section.

4.4.2 Reset Configuration Schemes

a) Loading default values during boot:

This is the most common reset configuration which does not require any special setup on board. It provides no flexibility or options to configure any register. All the registers are initialized to some fixed values and thus chip comes out only one fixed state after reset. This mode provides fastest mode to initialize the system before the boot process but is least powerful in terms of capabilities to control the system state. This might work for some applications but if same microcontroller is used in variety of application with varying boot requirement, this mode would be least preferred.

Figure 4-2 shows the timing diagram for this mode. System POR asserts internal chip Reset (both active low), when de-asserted restarts the clock and load reset configuration in the system registers. Based on system configuration the process might be gated with other necessary tasks (for example system to wait for PLL to get locked) before internal reset gets de-asserted and system starts to execute the boot code.

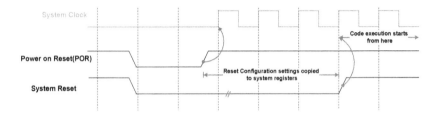

Figure 4-2: Loading default values during Reset

b) Fuse Programming:

This design scheme involves reset configuration that is generated from programming fuses or on-chip flash non-volatile registers in special test mode of operation of the chip. In this mode, special bits and registers are kept either in form of fuses or an array of nonvolatile registers in on-chip flash for configuring reset control word information. These registers need to have write-once capability and can only be programmed once in lifetime. Usually special setup or software is required to program these special registers or fuses. Once they are programmed, and a reset is issued to the microcontroller, the microcontroller would pick all the reset control word information from these special registers and copy them in the desired system registers. Once this is done, system de-asserts the reset internally and starts executing the software code. This scheme provides a lot of flexibility to configure different options in the system registers but at the cost of special fuse registers implementation in the design.

Figure 4-3: Reset Configuration bits from fuses or On-chip Flash

Figure 4-3 shows the reset configuration scheme. Note that since the fuses are one time programmable and this secure, these can very effectively utilized to enable and disable functions within the chip and phantom parts with lower price. This strategy is very common across semiconductor vendors that sell same silicon with different feature set (by blowing the fuses to enable/disable specific function) and cost.

c) Reset Configuration through External Pins:

This scheme includes group of pins on the microcontroller that controls the reset configuration. These special pins on the controller are pulled high or low externally during reset to define certain configuration. Once the system reset is de-asserted the microcontroller latches these values inside and decodes these values to configure the system configuration registers. This scheme provides limited flexibility in terms of selecting different control word configuration. Available number of configurations is directly proportional to the number of pins dedicated for this purpose. Usually this is done by having an external buffer or line driver like 74LVC125 that drives either "Logic 1" or "Logic 0" to the pins dedicated for reset configuration [17] (Figure 4-4).

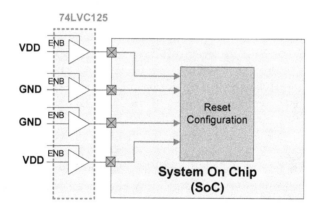

Figure 4-4: Reset Configuration through External Pins

Note that usually reset signal is connected to the enable of tristate buffer(external line driver) so any change ("Logic 1" or "Logic 0") to the input of tristate buffer is reflected as input to the pins that eventually go as reset configuration. This approach provides lot of flexibility and control. For example if one of the buffers control whether PLL will be enabled or disabled during boot, one of the buffer output can act as control that would provide user the ability to enable the PLL when buffer is connected to VDD and disable the PLL when buffer is connected to VSS.

Usually this approach is limited to the number of pins available for this purpose. Also note that most of the external line drivers (like 74LV125) comes in group of 4 or 8 buffers so in order to limit the cost of solution, it is advised to keep the number of buffers in multiples of 4.

d) Reset Configuration through external serial interface:

For a highly-integrated complex microprocessor it impractical to dedicate or to share pins for the numerous available power-up options. This scheme involves loading all the chip reset configuration data from external serial memory.

In a typical flow, when the system reset is asserted, chip establishes the serial communication with serial memory and reset configuration information is transferred from memory to microcontroller via serial communication. Once the serial data is received in microcontroller, it configures the system registers based on the received data and deasserts the reset. This method provides the maximum flexibility in terms of configuring different options in system registers as large number of data bytes can be written in serial memories. In some of the advanced serial configuration schemes, even software code can also be loaded in a serial memory. In this case, both reset configuration as well as boot code is read from external serial memory during microprocessor reset sequence and require only minimal I/O pins. By reading data stored in for example external SPI memory, the system would also need to configure the SPI memory clock frequency setting, configurable power-up options for the microprocessor, and optionally loads code into the microprocessor memory space. All this needs to be accomplished before the device's reset negates, ensuring the chip is properly configured when exiting the reset state.

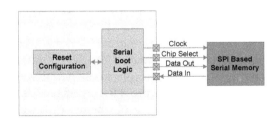

Figure 4-5: Reset Configuration through external SPI Serial Memory

Low cost of serial memories, simple implementation, high flexibility, along with optional software boot code makes it one of the most preferred option to boot or load reset configuration.

4.4.3 Boot from Interfaces

Figure 4-6 shows common hardware boot components that allow system to boot from variety of interfaces. Let's take a look at these options:-

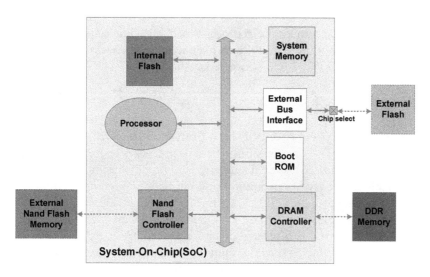

Figure 4-6: Hardware Boot Components

a) Boot from Internal Flash

This is one of the most common and simplest methods to boot an embedded microcontroller that includes the on-chip Flash. This method reduces dependencies on external interface since the bootloader resides in on-chip Flash. Processor after system reset deassertion points to the starting address of the on-chip Flash and loads the necessary initialization and OS. This is pretty popular way to boot a microcontroller that has a small OS footprint since there is a practical limitation on the amount of Flash that can be made available on-chip. Also this is one of most secure ways of booting the chip since the changes of modifying code residing is on-chip Flash is low as compared to off-chip boot options.

b) Boot from on-chip ROM

Just like Windows XP boot (As explained in Part I), some microcontrollers include boot ROM as the primary boot option. Boot ROM includes basic bootloader such that microcontroller can perform more sophisticated boot sequence on its own and load programs from various sources like Ethernet, NAND Flash, SD/MMC card, USB and so on. Boot ROM usage enables more flexible boot sequences than hardwired logic could provide and allows user the choice to boot from various peripherals. This feature is often used for system recovery purposes when for some reasons usual boot software in non-volatile memory (other than ROM) get erased.

Since Boot ROM cannot be reprogrammed, in some applications that require secure boot, Boot ROM may include security checks such that if a check fails during ROM boot, boot process is halted.

c) Boot from external bus interfaces

This allows the system to directly boot from external NOR Flash or other parallel memories. This offers one of the fastest ways to boot the system since the interface to external memory can be 32 bits or more with a reasonable frequency of operation. For a full-fledged operating system like Linux (or windows), it can take long time (several milliseconds to seconds) to boot the system due to size of Operating System (OS) that can be annoying to the user. Keeping the bootloader/OS in external parallel memory allows reducing the boot up time drastically for the systems where boot time is critical (for example in a medical equipment)

d) Boot from NAND Flash Controller

NAND Flash memories are gaining lot of popularity in customer applications like PDA, and mobile phone due to high throughput (but lower than NOR Flash), faster erase time and lower cost per Byte as compared to typical NOR Flash. Primary usage for NAND Flash is to store large quantities of data and code (for example USB Solid State Drives), however in the recent years there is an increase in number of embedded application that also support NAND Flash as primary boot option.

For supporting boot from NAND Flash, microcontroller must include NAND Flash controller to decode all the access to/from the NAND Flash. NAND flash interface require large number of pins (> 20 pins) so practically this option may not sound reasonable and cost effective unless a bigger pin count package is used.

e) Boot from Internal Memory (Volatile)

Boot from Internal memory is always part of Secondary boot since the RAM needs to be loaded by primary boot before it can execute the code. It is common to use one of the primary method of boot (as described in this section) to load the OS/Drivers and then copy the code to RAM. Once the OS is loaded into the RAM, it takes control of the system. Executing code from System RAM is faster and consumes less power than other memory technologies. This is much faster and efficient method than executing directly from External or Internal Flash. Since the internal RAM is volatile, some system allows the RAM to switch to battery supply in event of power failure so that there is no further need to copy the code from External/Internal Memory when the power comes back, thus reducing subsequent initialization/boot time.

f) Boot from DRAM

Booting from DRAM would always be a secondary boot where primary boot initializes DRAM driver to be able to execute the boot from. This is common for high end applications like phone or PlayStation that have to deal with lot of multimedia content and require high throughput. DRAM can be seen as bigger and faster extended RAM buffer that is required to manage complicated application.

Figure 4-7 shows one example of secondary boot using DRAM.

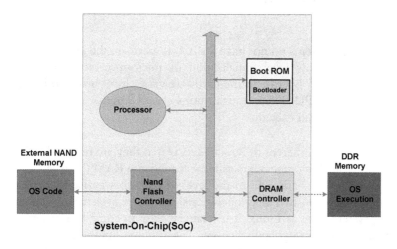

Figure 4-7: Secondary Boot with DRAM

In the example, ROM includes the boot loader while NAND Flash memory contains the OS and the application code. Boot process starts with system initialization in the ROM boot loader that also includes the reset vector. Main OS code is copied from the NAND Flash memory to DDR, thereby switching the execution control to external DDR after code in ROM is executed. This scheme is very efficient for multimedia as DDR is much faster than executing code from NAND Flash directly. Similar schemes can be used to copy the code from various interfaces like Ethernet etc.

f) Boot from various Peripherals

There may be a desire to boot from various interfaces like SDHC, SPI, I2C, USB, SATA, PCI Express, Ethernet and others. All this comes as part of secondary boot. As mentioned before, primary boot interface (like ROM) initializes secondary boot interface like USB before the code execution switches to secondary boot.

Storing boot code in external non-volatile serial memories like SPI Flash, EEPROM on IIC can be very useful for microcontrollers that have low pin count and can afford to have longer boot time. In this scheme, the boot code is first copied from the external memory to the On-chip RAM and code execution switches to the RAM just after the reset so that boot code can be fetched right after reset de-assertion.

4.5 Challenges on Embedded boot

Since embedded systems do not have a BIOS to perform the initial system configuration, the low level initialization of microprocessors, memory controllers, and other board-specific hardware varies from board to board and from CPU to CPU. These initializations must be performed before a Linux kernel image can execute.

Another complexity inherent in bootloaders is that they are required to be stored in nonvolatile storage but usually are loaded into RAM for execution. Again, the complexity arises from the level of resources available for the bootloader to rely on. In a fully operational computer system running an operating system such as Linux, it is relatively easy to compile a program and invoke it from nonvolatile storage. The runtime libraries, operating system, and compiler work together to create the infrastructure necessary to load a program from nonvolatile storage into memory and pass control to it. This infrastructure does not exist when a bootloader gains control upon power-on, which is generally the case in embedded systems. Instead, the bootloader must create its own operational context and move itself, if required, to a suitable location in RAM. Furthermore, additional complexity is introduced by the requirement to execute from a read-only medium.

4.6 Boot ROM

To provide more flexibility in boot, many processors include an on-chip "*Boot ROM*", typically multi-Kbyte that includes code that the processor vendor develops and burns into the ROM. As we'll see, the ROM code can perform many different functions.

One of the first tasks the ROM performs is to establish which boot mode has been selected. This is usually determined by reading the state of pins that have been tied high or low. These may be dedicated "Boot Mode Pins" or multipurpose I/O, depending on the processor as explained in Section 4.4.3. The ROM code reads the pin state and figures out which peripheral will be used to bring in the code and data. Alternatively other option is to make a selection via one time programmable memory (or fuses) which ROM can access and make a selection choice as previously explained in Section 4.4.3. The ROM code will then proceed to setup the peripheral interface, including the programming of all required registers, to make the transfer happen.

The ROM can also be responsible for setting default values of some important system parameters pertaining to memory initialization, interrupt handling and reset behavior. Because the ROM must be programmed to operate within a wide variety of system situations, it often uses only the "safest" values for key configurations like system and peripheral clock settings.

A series of headers usually "*frame*" the data on the memory device. The ROM first reads the header and then decodes it to decide how to proceed. These headers usually include parameters such as the number of bytes to be moved and the destination address of the transfer. One of the other useful header features is the ability to load a specific image based on certain board-level hardware. For example, a single product may have multiple configurations, from low-end to high-end. As such, the external flash may include multiple images to allow identical hardware to behave in different ways. The booting header can be used to select the desired executable out of this code store.

As with RAM, the boot ROM can be mapped at any memory level that the processor supports. Typically, these ROMs are located either in L1 memory level where instruction execution occurs in a single core clock cycle or in L3 memory level hierarchy, where execution occurs in the slower system clock domain. If a larger ROM is required, it is most often at the L3 level. If speed of execution is important, an L1 ROM is more appropriate.

4.7 Primary and secondary Bootloader

Broadly boot components can be classified into primary or secondary on the basis of the capability to support boot right after reset de-assertion.

Primary option provides a direct boot capability and facilitates the first instruction fetch of processor from the memory location where software initialization code resides. These interfaces are expected to be enabled and configured right after reset and can sometimes be configured through the reset configuration option (as explained in 4.4.2). Small software initialization code that resides in ROM is what constitutes the primary bootloader.

In many cases, the flexibility can be extended by the use of a secondary or 2nd stage bootloader that is simply code that is booted in by the Primary interface (for example boot ROM) to setup the system and bring in remaining code. Secondary interfaces are initialized and configured in these boot code/boot loaders which are placed at primary interfaces. They are mainly used to keep the large size OS kernel code which is loaded after basic initialization is performed by the boot loader. OS Kernel code can directly be executed from these interfaces or it can be copied to some memory which is accessible to the processor. The behavior is shown in Figure 4-8.

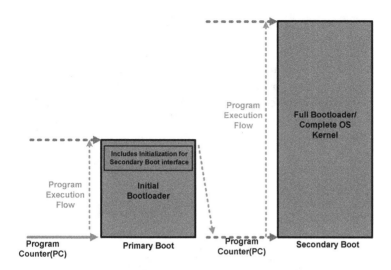

Figure 4-8: Primary and Secondary Boot Options

Practically Primary boot can be on-chip component like ROM that can include initial initialization code such that the execution switches to secondary option like external DDR that includes complete OS Kernel.

More often secondary bootloader could be a peripheral that is not natively supported by boot ROM. For example, peripherals that require a protocol may be difficult to implement in a boot ROM, for example Ethernet.

The simplest type of boot ROM may just look for a fixed size code block from external memory. This fixed size block almost always serves as a secondary bootloader. One good example of a 2nd stage loader is U-Boot, an open source, universal boot loader. It is a small segment of software that is brought in from external memory and executes soon after powering up a processor.

4.7.1 Universal Boot Loader (U-Boot)

There are many standard boot loaders used in embedded applications like DINK32, Open Firmware, and x86 bios etc. which facilitates the loading of an Operating System (OS) and bring the system in safe state. U-boot is one of the similar open source universal bootloader that is more popular, especially for Linux based embedded applications. U-Boot provides an automated interactive environment which offers user a lot of flexibility and options to choose among various different boot schemes and interfaces. It provides an excellent platform to the end application development user who doesn't need to go into low level specifics of the chip hardware. After basic initialization of system, it starts a user interactive program which allows user the capability to provide their input (for example the interface system wants to boot from can be part of input) through a serial communication interface console utility like HyperTerminal in windows. Note that a user can also choose to run U-Boot without any intervention in an automated way and that's how it is used in the final application [17].

U-Boot can reside in internal ROM or Flash. After the basic CPU, local memories, bus initialization, U-Boot can relocate itself to a RAM location and then executes from there. Figure 4-9 shows the splash screen that is displayed on serial console when U-Boot is running.

```
U-Boot 1.1.6 (SEPT 10 2010 - 19:08:47) MPCXXXX
Clock configuration:
 Coherent System Bus:  166 MHz
 Core:                 333 MHz
 Local Bus Controller: 166 MHz
 Local Bus:            33 MHz
 DDR:                  333 MHz
 SEC:                  55 MHz
 I2C1:                 166 MHz
 I2C2:                 166 MHz
 TSEC1:                166 MHz
 TSEC2:                166 MHz
 USB MPH:              0 MHz
 USB DR:               55 MHz
CPU: MPCXXXXX, Rev: 10 at 333.333 MHz
Board: Freescale MPCXXXXXX
I2C:   ready
DRAM:  Initializing
DDR RAM: 128 MB
FLASH: 8 MB
NAND:  32 MiB
In:    serial
Out:   serial
Err:   serial
Net:   TSEC0, TSEC1
Hit any key to stop autoboot: 0
=>
```

Figure 4-9: U-Boot Splash Screen

U-Boot supports a very powerful set of commands which can be executed through the interactive command window. Other than loading OS, these commands provide lot of functions like memory load/dump, serial interface access and read/erase/program functions for external memories like NAND, NOR, Serial Flash and EEPROM. U-boot allows the system to boot from variety of interfaces like USB, SD, PCIe, SATA, etc.

117

Figure 4-10 shows the U-Boot command set classification that is categorized based on the functionality.

- Information Commands (**help, bdiinfo** etc)
- Memory Commands (**crc32, mtest** etc)
- Flash Memory Commands (**erase, protect, cp** etc)
- Execution Control Commands (**autoscr, go, bootm** etc)
- Network Commands (**tftpboot, dhcp, ping** etc)
- Environment Variables Commands (**setenv, run** etc)
- Filesystem Support Commands (**chpart, ls, fsload** etc)
- Special Commands (**regdump, i2c** etc)
- Miscellaneous Commands (**reset, echo** etc)

Figure 4-10: U-Boot Command Set Classification

For more details, U-Boot development resources can be referred at http://sourceforge.net/projects/u-boot/ and http://www.denx.de/wiki/U-Boot/

Another point worth mentioning is that U-Boot being an open source bootloader, embedded developers are contributing heavily on U-Boot environment adding lot device support keeping U-Boot rich and up-to-date.

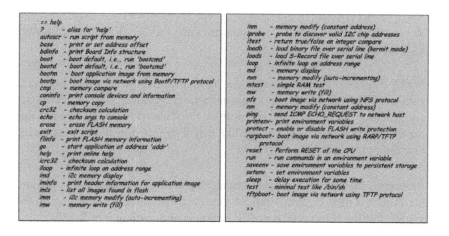

Figure 4-11: U-Boot Command Set

To load an OS in a typical scheme over a network(for example Ethernet), U-Boot first initializes all the network environment variables and then copy the OS kernel image to the target board and then jumps the execution to the OS Kernel. After this point, U-Boot plays no role anywhere in the system. Apart from Ethernet, U-Boot also supports OS kernel boot from various different advanced interfaces like NAND Flash, PCI, PCI-Express, USB, SATA etc. U-boot image size is generally dependent on the boot peripheral support selected at the compile or build time of U-Boot source code. For different applications, U-Boot features can be customized to suit the need appropriately.

U-Boot follows a standardized directory structure which allows high scalability and portability to different platforms. While porting the U-Boot for any new platform, most of the files remain same other than CPU, new peripherals and board specific files. All these powerful features make U-Boot a desired choice for embedded developers.

4.8 Embedded Boot Examples

4.8.1 Router Boot (CISCO)

Router goes through the following three steps during boot

  a) Power On Self-Test (POST)
  b) Locate and load OS
  c) Locate and run device configuration file

Router *Boot ROM* stores four components POST, Bootstrap program, ROMMON mode and Mini IOS.

POST (Power on self-test) is a low level diagnostic utility that performs various tests on hardware components. It verifies that all necessary components are present and operational. Modular slots are checked in this process for any hardware change like installing new interface or removing existing interfaces.

Bootstrap is the second utility in booting sequence. It controls the search and load process of IOS. Bootstrap program is responsible for bringing up the router, finding IOS on all possible locations and loading it in RAM.

ROMMON is a portable IOS program that allows system to perform various diagnostic tests. This program is also used for password recovery procedure. It has its own mode known as ROMMON mode. Boot sequence follows a conditional rule for this mode. If bootstrap successes in finding and loading operation of IOS, than boot sequence will not enter in this mode. Boot sequence will enter in this mode automatically, if it fails to load IOS in RAM from all possible locations [18]. One can manually enter in this mode for diagnostic purpose by running reload command from privileged mode to reboot the router, mostly commonly this is associated with pressing CTRL + C key combination in first 60 seconds of boot sequence.

Mini-IOS is a fallback utility that contains a stripped down version of IOS. This is used in critical situations where IOS image in flash is not found. Mini-IOS contains only IP code that allows to load IOS from other resources such as TFTP Server. Cisco IOS mode used by this stripped down IOS utility known as RXBOOT mode [18].

The non-volatile code is stored in external Flash, Boot ROM during the boot process copies IOS image from the Flash to internal SRAM.

Router also include NVRAM that is used to store data such as configuration parameters so data is not lost when router is powered off.

Router RAM is part of SoC and is a temporary memory. Information stored in RAM does not remain in power off stage. Everything in RAM is erased, when you turn off the router. RAM is the fastest memory among these memories. In a powered on router, RAM contains all the information required to function the device.

5. System Integrity

5.1 Introduction

Embedded electronic control units are finding their way into more and more complex safety critical and mission critical applications. Many of these applications operate in adverse conditions, which can cause code runaway in the embedded control systems, putting them into unknown states. A watchdog timer is the best way to bring the system out of an unknown state into a safe state. Given its importance, the watchdog has to be carefully designed, so as to reduce the chances of its operation being compromised by runaway code. This chapter outlines the need for robust Watchdog and the guidelines that must be considered while designing a fault tolerant system monitor aka Watchdog. Efficient methods for refreshing a watchdog, write protection mechanism, early detection of code runaway and a quick self-test of the watchdog have been described in this chapter.

5.2 The Need for fault tolerant systems

Electronic control units (ECU) are fast becoming ubiquitous. Among other areas, they are increasingly finding their way into safety critical and mission critical applications, such as automobile safety systems, aircraft fly-by-wire controls and spacecraft thrust controls. These control systems are supposed to work reliably under all environmental conditions. The software, running on the ECU, does experience faults while running in the real environment which may lead to partial or total system crash. Therefore it is of utmost importance that the system must display a high degree of fault tolerance, so that if and when faults like software crashes happen, it is able to recover quickly and bring itself into a safe state.

A good example of a mission and safety critical application is the thrust control of a spacecraft. One of the most delicate operations carried out in outer space is the docking of two spacecraft's. Precision direction control and maneuvers are required to line up the two bodies properly, so that they can dock. The system controlling the spacecraft's thrusters must work flawlessly. A software crash in the thrusters' ECU could result in the thrusters firing away for too long, or at the wrong angle, or both, and instead of a docking a collision would result. A safety mechanism must be in place that can detect faults and put the ECU into a safe state before the thrusters start firing away unpredictably [19].

Another critical application is that of robotic arms in surgeries, which are becoming common in advanced medical facilities. These systems can enhance the ability of physicians to perform complex procedures with minimum interventions. During an operation, the physician initiates a particular procedure, say a fine incision in a vital organ, and then control goes completely to the robotic arm wielding the scalpel. If software failure happens while the robot is at work, the robotic arm could behave unpredictably, posing a risk to the patient. If there is ability in the system to recover quickly from such crashes, the robotic operation can halt and the physician can take appropriate further actions. The operating room of the future is envisioned as a fully automated cell. The surgery would be carried out by robotic arms, under remote supervision from any place around globe. Then fault-tolerance becomes much more critical owing to the increased system dependency.

The above examples serve to highlight the need for fault tolerant systems. Looking ahead, it's not just the automotive, industrial, aeronautical, medical and space applications that need fault tolerance. With the introductions of the IEC 60730 standards, it is required that even automatic electronic controls in household appliances ensure safe and reliable operation of their component.

5.3 Reasons for System Failure

When deployed in any application, embedded systems experience two kinds of failures, hard errors and soft errors. Hard errors signify irreversible damage to the system, for example permanent damage to the chip package due to excessive vibrations in a machine, or internal transistor breakdown at extreme temperatures. On the other hand, it is possible for the system to recover from soft errors. Soft errors generally involve some form of data corruption in the system. Reasons could vary from cosmic ray exposure, EMI, noisy power supply to faulty coding. Cosmic rays or other kinds of high frequency radiations would be conditions commonly faced by space crafts and controls in X-ray units of hospitals. The robotic arm in the surgery unit is a pertinent example as it can be exposed to stray radiations from X-ray units. With increasing system frequencies, on chip high speed serial interfaces and decreasing pitch of chip package pins, EMI is an all too familiar enemy. Power supplies to the chip can be held hostage to transients at the time of power down and can face droop due to ground bounce or current surge. Cosmic rays can cause bit-flipping in memory bit cells, while EMI and noisy power supplies can result in a read or write of incorrect data to memories/registers.

When such data corruption happens, program execution can get affected as the program counter might have gotten modified. Modification of the program code memory or a read of wrong data from code memory can result in a totally different and unintended instruction getting executed. Thus, program flow or the program code itself gets modified, i.e. code runaway, and the system can enter an unknown state where its behavior is unpredictable. Such runaway can also be a result of faulty coding on part of the firmware coder. There might be unhandled exceptions, out of bound array accesses, unbounded loops or simply an unexpected sequence of user inputs, all of which can lead to an unexpected outcome.

Once the program flow takes an unexpected branch, the system can start behaving unpredictably, which is unacceptable for a safety critical system. For example, an airbag control unit could go haywire, firing at the wrong time or worse, not firing during an accident. While there are remedial measures available to prevent data corruption, there is need for a system monitor that can detect such system failures and take action to bring the system into a safe/known state. The system monitor would, in essence, act as the last "*dive-and-catch*" for the system when a code runaway takes place. The system monitor should be able to reliably detect a code runaway and then bring the system into a safe state with minimum delay. The system monitor should itself be immune to code runaways.

5.4 A System Monitor – The Watchdog Timer

For quite some time now, the role of a system monitor in embedded systems has been fulfilled by a simple piece of logic called the Watchdog. It is known by different names - COP (Computer Operating Properly), Watchdog Timer or simply Watchdog. It is essentially a timer running off a continuous clock. It expects to receive some sort of an "All's well" signal from the system at regular intervals. This signaling is termed as "refreshing the watchdog", and can take varied forms depending on the implementation – for example, a write of a particular value by the system's CPU to a designated location in the watchdog's register space, or the execution of a special instruction by the CPU. In the absence of such a signal, the watchdog timer eventually times out and issues a reset to the system. The minimum frequency at which the watchdog has to be refreshed is determined by the timeout value of its timer. Figure 5-1 illustrates the basic concept of a watchdog.

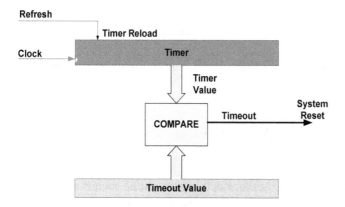

Figure 5-1: Concept of a Watchdog

The way that the aforementioned arrangement works is that the firmware code is first profiled to determine the sequence of instruction execution and the time taken. Watchdog refresh routines are then inserted into the code, in such a manner that the interval between the executions of two successive refresh routines works out to be less than the watchdog timer's timeout period. If a code runaway happens, the program flow will get disrupted and either the refresh routines won't be executed at all or they would be executed at intervals exceeding the timeout period. The watchdog timer would timeout and reset the system, pulling it back into a known state.

One essential requirement of a watchdog is that it should be immune to the effects of runaway code. If runaway code was to accidentally disable the watchdog, then there would be no way for the system to recover. Even a similar modification in other parameters of the watchdog, such as its timeout period, is undesired. Therefore a lot of thought has to go into the design of a watchdog and also its integration into the system.

5.4.1 Designing a good Watchdog

To design a good watchdog the following guidelines should be kept mind [19]:

• The width of the watchdog timer should be such that it can cover a whole range of timeout's, for all available clock sources in the system.

• The watchdog timer should run off a clock source that is independent of the clock source of the system that it is monitoring. Preferably it should be a dedicated clock source for the watchdog, say an RC oscillator. This means that even if the system clock dies out due to some reason, leaving the system hung, the watchdog timer can still timeout and reset the system.

• The watchdog's method of signaling a fault to the system should be fault tolerant itself.

• The critical control and configuration register bits of the watchdog should have write protection on them so that once set they cannot be accidentally modified.

• The method of refreshing the watchdog should be such that the chances of runaway code accidentally refreshing the watchdog are minimal. If runaway code, through some weird chance, manages to refresh the watchdog, the watchdog would either not get to know about the code runaway or get to know it after a long time.

• The response of the watchdog to detection of runaway condition should be swift. If the watchdog takes too much time to reset the system, the system in an unknown state could cause a lot of damage in a safety critical application. Thinking back to the example of the robotic arm, the longer it takes for the arm to be halted in case of a fault, the more risk there is to the patient's life.

• The watchdog's proper operation should be testable so that it can be made sure after boot that it is up and functioning. The test should not take an impractical amount of time.

• The watchdog should facilitate diagnosis of the fault that caused a watchdog timeout.

NOTE: *All recommended features that an ideal watchdog must include is described as "Robust Watchdog" within this chapter.*

5.5 Robust Watchdog

A Robust Watchdog has to be designed keeping in mind the aforementioned guidelines. It should incorporate the features that make improvements over existing implementations, in the following specific areas:

• Better, more unique, timed refresh scheme.
• Timed password style access to control and configuration registers.
• Detection of runaway code footprints, before actual timeout.
• Faster but at the same time fault tolerant response to timeouts.
• Fast test of the watchdog.

5.5.1 The Width of Watchdog Timer

When designing a watchdog, one of the questions confronting the designer is how wide the watchdog timer should be kept. The answer to this can be obtained by deciding on what range of timeout values does one want to support and then considering the different clocks available to the watchdog.

Consider an example target timeout range of 1ms to 1 second. To be able to generate timeout values ranging from 1ms to 1 second, the length of the watchdog timer has to be chosen carefully. What makes this task difficult is that the frequency of the clock source for the watchdog could vary widely from a few KHz (say an on-chip RTC oscillator) to hundreds of MHz (system clock). Figure 5-2 shows timeout values possible with 8, 16, 24 and 32 bit timers, for different, practical clock frequencies.

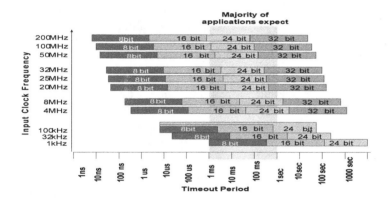

Figure 5-2: Possible Timeouts [20] (Log Scale)

The vertical band marks out a range of timeouts which cover the 1ms to 1 second range. As can be observed, a 32 bit counter is required to cover all clock frequencies and the expected range of watchdog timeouts.

126

5.5.2 Independent Clock Source

A Robust Watchdog should implement a pretty standard option of switching between two clock inputs, one of which should ideally be connected to a dedicated clock source, such as an on-chip RC oscillator. The other clock source can be the system clock. In applications which aren't safety critical but still need the watchdog, the system designer might want to avoid the overhead of a dedicated clock source and simply use the system clock.

5.5.3 Write Protection

Watchdogs generally have several control and configuration register bits, which are used to influence its working, for example a bit to disable or enable the watchdog. Since these bits have a direct impact on the watchdog's functioning, it is of prime interest to make sure they are not modified un-intentionally. To achieve this objective a write protection scheme is generally present in good watchdogs. One of the better, extant, write-protection schemes is to have a password style protection on the said register bits, where the password is a sequence of two particular values. However, this scheme allows any amount of time to elapse in between the write of the two values, which means that the chances of runaway code managing to accidentally replicate the password are high. If the writes of the two values are spaced far apart in the code, it could so happen that after the write of the first value the code runs away in an unintended direction, causes havoc, and then after enough number of iterations, branches to the location of the write of the second value.

A Robust Watchdog should place a restriction on the time gap between the writes of the two values, thereby reducing chances of runaway code being able to "*unlock*" the registers for writing and possibly disabling the watchdog. By placing a limit on the time gap, where the limit is just equal to the time it takes for the CPU to fetch and execute the write instruction for the second value, the user is forced to place the write instructions for the two values one after the other in the code (as assembly instructions). Now if there is a runaway after the execution of the first write, there is no time left for the code to possibly return and execute the instruction writing the second value of the sequence. This makes the refresh sequence more unique because it minimizes the chance of the sequence being replicated by runaway code.

If the gap between the two words of the password is more than a few system bus clock cycles, the watchdog infers an exception and resets the system. In addition, the amount of time for which the registers stay "unlocked" is limited too, roughly equal to the time it takes for these registers to be configured once, after which they are "locked" again. This write protection is in effect from right after system reset, leaving no room for runaway code to "sneak in" and change the watchdog's configuration.

5.5.4 Unique Refresh Scheme

Refresh schemes exist in various flavors, a simple write of a particular value (say 0x35), the execution of a refresh instruction that is part of the processor's instruction set, or the write of a sequence of two values in a particular order (say 0xAA followed by 0x55). A Robust Watchdog's refresh scheme should include a sequence of two values, but is different from other watchdogs in that it should place a limit on the time that can elapse between the write of the two values. If the first value of the sequence is written and not followed by the second one within a certain number of system bus clock cycles, the watchdog infers an exception and resets the system. The reasoning behind this scheme is similar to that for the password style write protection scheme described in previous section. The restriction on the time gap between the writes of the two values is intended to preclude a situation where there is a code runaway and there is an accidental refresh of the watchdog, preventing it from resetting the system. Also, particular care has been taken to not choose values like 0x55 and 0xAA for the refresh sequence, since these are commonly used in memory write-then-read software tests. Such tests are sometimes part of the boot code which means there would be multiple instances of these values in the code. Having these same values as refresh sequence for the watchdog increases the probability of an accidental refresh during code runaway.

5.5.5 Windowed Refresh

A Robust Watchdog should have an option for a windowed refresh, as opposed to the normal refresh. Again, this is a pretty standard feature, available in most existing implementations. The principle behind the windowed refresh is that watchdog can be refreshed only in a particular window of its timeout period. In a Robust Watchdog, this window should be defined by points in time, in between the timeout period and at the end of the timeout period. If the refresh takes place outside the window, this is a sign that the program code execution is taking place faster than expected and hence points to something abnormal in program code execution [19]. Figure 5-3 illustrates the concept of windowed refreshing.

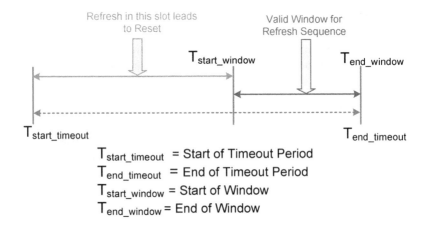

$$T_{start\_timeout} = \text{Start of Timeout Period}$$
$$T_{end\_timeout} = \text{End of Timeout Period}$$
$$T_{start\_window} = \text{Start of Window}$$
$$T_{end\_window} = \text{End of Window}$$

Figure 5-3: Windowed Mode of Refresh

5.5.6 Fast Response to Code Runaway

As has been emphasized before, it is imperative that the response of the watchdog to code runaway be fast. Code runaway is a state in which the system acts in-deterministically and so it should be brought out of that state as fast as possible. A Robust Watchdog should take a proactive approach to this problem.

While the method of running a timer in the watchdog and interpreting its timeout as a sign of system failure (due to runaway code or system clock failure) is time tested, it does however have once shortcoming. If code runaway happens in the early stages of the watchdog timer period, it takes a lot of time before safety measures (like resetting the system) kick in, because the watchdog waits for its timer to timeout. In some applications, this delay in the watchdog reacting, might be as large as 1 second (the watchdog's timeout period). A Robust Watchdog should seek to do this by recognizing the signs of runaway code early on and resetting the system immediately, without waiting for a timeout of its internal timer. These signs are:

• Presence of a value, other than the two bonafide values of the refresh sequence or the register-unlock password, in the watchdog's refresh or unlock register - The user's software code would only contain instruction writing the said sets of two values to these registers. Thus, the presence of a third value indicates something abnormal happening in the code, probably due to a runaway.

• Failure to write to configuration registers within a small, fixed amount of time after unlocking them - Again, this indicates something abnormal as a normal user code would contain at least one watchdog configuration operation following the instructions which unlock the registers.

• Failure to write to at least one of the configuration registers within a small, fixed amount of time after system reset de-assertion - This might seem an overkill but by forcing the user to do so, it is ensured that the user doesn't forget to properly configure the watchdog and get it up and running, as per the system's needs, as soon as possible after reset, in the midst all the other boot up tasks that are required by the system.

When indeed a timeout takes place, the logic generating a reset to the system is run off the fast system clock (in the range of tens to hundreds of MHz), rather than the watchdog's dedicated, slow clock (in the range of a few KHz to a few MHz). If the reset were to be generated off the slow clock, say 1 KHz, it could take the watchdog almost 1ms to reset the system, after timeout, leaving too much time for run-away code to cause havoc. One risk in generating the reset off the system clock is that in the event this clock fails, the watchdog timer's timeout would go unacknowledged and wouldn't reset the system. To take care of such a situation, a backup circuit in the Robust Watchdog waits for second consecutive timeout of timer and passes it on as reset to the system, as shown in Figure 5-4 [19].

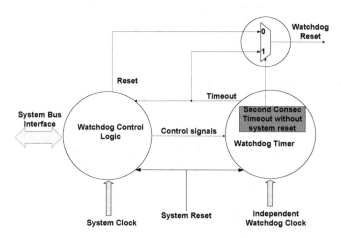

Figure 5-4: Reset Generation Logic

5.5.7 Testing the Watchdog in Reduced Time

For IEC 60730 and other safety standards the expectation is that anything that monitors a safety function must be tested and this test is required to be fault tolerant. To test the watchdog, its main timer and its associated compare and reset logic should be tested. Most current implementations of the watchdog do a simple overflow test of their timers. A 32 bit timer running on a 1 KHz clock would take ~4×10^6 seconds to overflow, which is unreasonably long for a test. For a Robust Watchdog, during its test, the timer should split up into its constituent byte-wide stages, which are then run independently and tested for timeout against the corresponding byte of the actual timeout value. The following block diagram, in Figure 5-5, explains the "splitting" concept. Here the case is shown for the test of Byte Stage 3 of the timer.

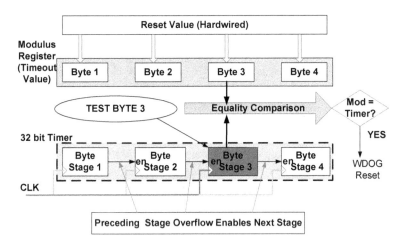

Figure 5-5: Robust Watchdog Test Scheme

Each stage is an 8-bit synchronous counter followed by combinational logic which generates an Overflow signal. The Overflow signal acts as an enable to the N+1th stage [19].

In test mode, when an individual byte is selected to be tested, say byte N, then bytes 0 to N-1 are force loaded with 0xFF, and byte N is allowed to run off the clock source. By doing so the Overflow signal from stage N-1 is generated immediately, enabling counter stage N. The Nth stage runs and compares with the Nth byte of the timeout value register. This way byte N is tested, as well the link between it and the preceding stage. None of the other stages, N-2, N-3….and N+1, N+2…..are enabled for the test on byte

131

N. These disabled stages (except the most significant stage of the counter) are loaded with a value of 0xFF. For a 1 KHz clock, a test of each byte, one after another, would take 4x 256ms (~103ms) for a 32 bit timeout value set to all 1's, i.e. 0xFFFFFFFF [19]. The actual time taken would depend on the actual timeout value that is set.

5.5.8 Count of Watchdog Resets

A Robust Watchdog should also keep a count of the number of times it reset the system. This count is made visible to the software through a register, which is reset only on a Power-on-Reset. If this count reaches a certain threshold, the system might want to interpret it as an extra-ordinary situation and take some action over and above its normal reaction to a watchdog reset.

Increasing involvement of embedded electronic controls in safety critical and mission critical applications means that an increased fault tolerance is required in these embedded systems. A system monitor, that can independently monitor software execution and safe-state the system in the event of a code runaway, is a crucial part of these systems. The watchdog timer has been serving this function for a long time. The Robust Watchdog improves upon existing watchdog implementations by making small but important changes in the refresh scheme, the write protection of configuration and control registers and the testing of the watchdog timer. It also detects code runaway as early as possible and reacts to it in the least possible amount of time. On the whole, the Robust Watchdog has more immunity to its operation being compromised by code runaway, compared to existing implementations.

6. *Debouncing Techniques*

6.1 Introduction

When any two metal contacts in an electronic device to generate multiple signals as the contacts close or open is known as *"Bouncing"*. *"Debouncing"* is any kind of hardware device or software that ensures that only a single signal will be acted upon for a single opening or closing of a contact.

Mechanical Switch and relay contacts are usually made of springy metals that are forced into contact by an actuator. When the contacts strike together, their momentum and elasticity act together to cause bounce. The result is a rapidly pulsed electrical current instead of a clean transition from zero to full current. The waveform is then further modified by the parasitic inductances and capacitances in the switch and wiring, resulting in a series of damped sinusoidal oscillations. This effect is usually unnoticeable in AC mains circuits, where the bounce happens too quickly to affect most equipment, but causes problems in some analogue and logic circuits that respond fast enough to misinterpret the on-off pulses as a data stream.

Sequential digital logic circuits are particularly vulnerable to contact bounce. The voltage waveform produced by switch bounce usually violates the amplitude and timing specifications of the logic circuit. The result is that the circuit may fail, due to problems such as metastability, race conditions, runt pulses and glitches.

When you press a key on your computer keyboard, you expect a single contact to be recorded by your computer. In fact, however, there is an initial contact, a slight bounce or lightening up of the contact, then another contact as the bounce ends, yet another bounce back, and so forth. Usually Manufactures for these use Membrane switches that includes a sheet of rubber with a tip of rubberized conductive material that when pressed makes a connection with a set of exposed contacts on the circuit board. The rubber is soft therefore provides a soft connection that has little to no bounce. The main problem is that most of these solutions don't stand up very well to the high impact stress of being stepped on.

This chapter details on de-bouncing techniques and guidelines for design consideration in order to have a smooth bounce free switch.

6.2 Behavior of a Switch

Figure 6-1 shows a simple push switch with a pull-up resistor. Figure 6-2 shows the corresponding output when the switch is pressed and released.

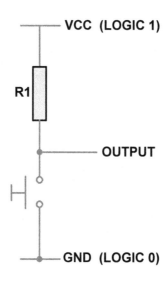

Figure 6-1: Push Switch with Pull-Up Resistor

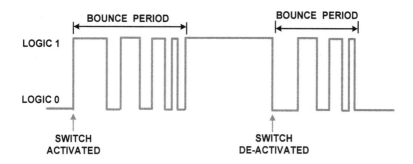

Figure 6-2: Bounce Period during Switch Activation and de-activation

If the switch is used to turn on a lamp or start a fan motor, then contact bounce is not a problem. But if the switch or relay is used as input to a digital counter, a personal computer, or a micro-processor based piece of equipment, then it may cause issues due to the contact bounce. The counter would get multiple counts rather than the expected single count. Same problem exists when the switch is released.

The reason for concern is due to the fact that the time it takes for contacts to stop bouncing is typically in the order of milliseconds while digital circuits can respond in microseconds or even faster (in nanoseconds).

The usual solution is a de-bouncing device or software that ensures that only one digital signal can be registered within the space of a given time (usually milliseconds). Before jumping to various solutions for de-bouncing a switch, let's understand couple of switches and the bounce period.

6.3 Switch Types

The simplest type of switch is one where two electrical conductors are brought in contact with each other by the motion of an actuating mechanism. Other switches are more complex, containing electronic circuits able to turn on or off depending on some physical stimulus (such as light or magnetic field) sensed. In any case, the final output of any switch will be (at least) a pair of wire-connection terminals that will either be connected together by the switch's internal contact mechanism ("*closed*"), or not connected together ("*open*").

Some of the switches are shown in Figure 6-3.

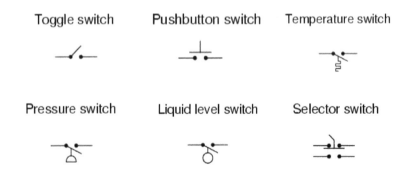

Figure 6-3: Types of Switches

Toggle switches are actuated by a lever angled in one of two or more positions. The common light switch used in household wiring is an example of a toggle switch.

Pushbutton switches are two-position devices actuated with a button that is pressed and released. Most pushbutton switches have an internal spring mechanism returning the button to its *"out,"* or *"un-pressed,"* position, for momentary operation.

Temperature switch consists of a thin strip of two metals, joined back-to-back, each metal having a different rate of thermal expansion. When the strip heats or cools, differing rates of thermal expansion between the two metals causes it to bend. The bending of the strip can then be used to actuate a switch contact mechanism.

For a pressure switch, gas or liquid pressure can be used to actuate a switch mechanism if that pressure is applied to a piston, diaphragm, or bellows, which converts pressure to mechanical force.

Level switches can also be designed to detect the level of solid materials such as wood chips, grain, coal etc.

Selector switches are actuated with a rotary knob or lever of some sort to select one of two or more positions. Like the toggle switch, selector switches can either rest in any of their positions or contain spring-return mechanisms for momentary operation.

There may be many more switches not listed here but different switches may behave differently and may exhibit different bounce period. A simple cheap switch may exhibit a higher bounce period than a switch designed for specific purpose for example a switch designed with multiple parallel contacts give less bounce, but at greater switch complexity and cost. There are various techniques and guidelines for a switch design that can be considered to reduce the bounce period but this is beyond the scope of this book.

6.4 De-bouncing Techniques

There are several ways to solve the problem of contact bounce (that is, to "de-bounce" the input signal). The section mentions both hardware and software solutions to solve the problem.

6.4.1 RC De-bouncer

A Resistor-Capacitor (RC) network is probably the most common and easiest method of de-bouncing circuit. It is simply a resistor and capacitor wired together with the switch connected to the central connection as shown in Figure 6-4. The capacitor is charged through the resistor, so the default state when the switch is not engaged is high. When the switch is engaged, it slowly drains the capacitor to ground thus softening any small bounces. The circuit may sustain some bounce but it doesn't eliminate it completely (Figure 6-5).

When the switch is opened, the voltage across the capacitor is zero, but it starts to climb at a rate determined by the values of R and C. Bouncing contacts pull the voltage down and slow the cap's charge accumulation. A very slow discharging R/C ratio is required to eliminate the bounces completely. R/C can be adjusted to a value such that voltage stays below a gate's logic one level till bouncing stops. This has a potential side-effect that switch may not respond to fast *"open"* and *"close"* if the time constant is too long.

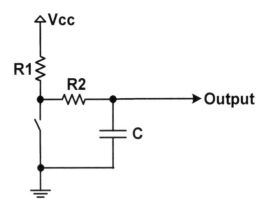

Figure 6-4: A RC De-bouncer

Now, suppose the switch has been open for a while. The capacitor is fully charged. The user closes the switch, which discharges the capacitor through R2. Slowly, again, the voltage drops down and the gate continues to see a logic one at its input for a time. Here the contacts open and close for a small time during the bouncing. While open, even if only for short periods, the two resistors start to recharge the cap, reinforcing the logic one to the gate. Again, component values can be chosen such that it guarantees the gate sees a one until the bouncing contacts settle.

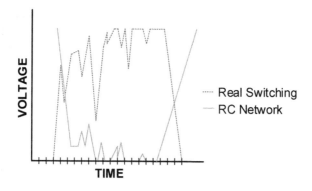

Figure 6-5: Real switching vs. RC Network

RC circuit shown above works well to eliminate any bounces even without having R2 (R2 = 0). Switch operating at high speed may have bounces in the order of sub-microseconds or less thus having sharp rise times. To make things worse, depending on the physical arrangement of the components, the input to the switch might go to a logic zero while the voltage across the capacitor is still one. When the contacts bounce open the gate now sees a one. The output is a train of ones and zeroes bounces. R2 insures the capacitor discharges slowly, giving a clean logic level regardless of the frequency of bounces. The resistor also limits current flowing through the switch's contacts, so they aren't burned up by a momentary major surge of electrons from the capacitor.

Lastly, the state information coming from the switch is not digital in nature, so to control something like a switching IC with this won't work very well. In order to use the switch state information properly a basic analog-to-digital conversion is required. This comprises of a logic gate tacked on to the RC network as shown in Figure 6-6.

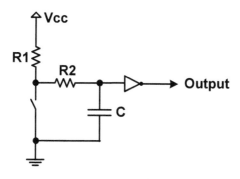

Figure 6-6: RC Network with Digital Logic

The logic gate has a certain voltage threshold at which it changes its output state. This provides some more tolerance to switch bounce but switch bounce can still leak through as shown in Figure 6-7.

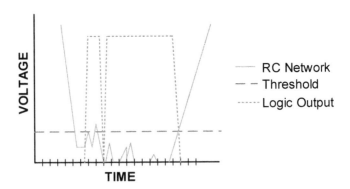

Figure 6-7: RC Network vs Logic Output

The logic gate or the inverter cannot be a standard logic gate. For instance TTL Logic defines a zero as an input between 0.0 and 0.8 volts and a one when input is more than 2.0 volts. In between 0.8 V and 2.0V the output is unpredictable. Some more bounce tolerance can be added by using logic gates with Schmitt triggers. With a Schmitt trigger when the voltage drops below the first threshold it will not switch state again, even if the voltage crosses the same threshold, until the other higher threshold is reached. This will reduce the sensitivity the Schmitt triggered gate has for switch bounce. The behavior is shown in Figure 6-8.

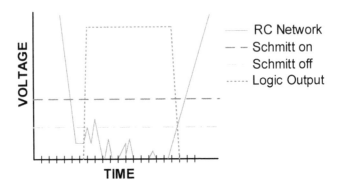

Figure 6-8: RC Network vs. Logic Output (Schmitt)

Circuits based on "*Schmitt trigger*" inputs have hysteresis, the inputs can dither yet the output remains in a stable, known state.

It can be pretty annoying trying to adjust RC ratio for each and every circuit. Let's come up with generic RC circuit that works for all cases.

Discharging of a Capacitor is defined as

$$V_{Cap} = V_{initial}(e^{-t/RC})$$

where
V_{Cap} = Voltage across the capacitor at time t
$V_{initial}$ = Initial voltage across the capacitor
t = time in seconds
R = Value of the resistor in Ohms
C = Value of the Capacitor in Farads

Values of R and C should be selected in such a way that V_{Cap} always stays above the threshold voltage at which the gate switches till switch stops bouncing.

R1 + R2 controls the capacitor charge time, and sets the debounce period for the condition where the switch opens. The equation for charging is:

$$V_{threshold} = V_{final}(1 - e^{-t/RC})$$

where
$V_{threshold}$ = Worst case transition point voltage across the capacitor
V_{final} = Final charged value across the capacitor

Figure 6-9 shows a small change to the RC de-bounce that includes a diode between R1 and R2. Diode is an optional component here and takes care of correct operation even when a hysteresis voltage assumes different values due to wrong gate such that value of R1 + R2 comes out to be less than R2. In this case, the diode forms a short cut that removes R2 from the charging circuit. All of the charge flows through R1.

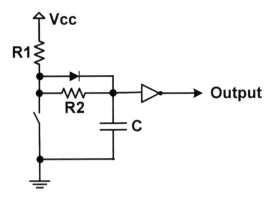

Figure 6-9: Robust RC debounce circuit

Let's analyze this in more details. Figure 6-10 shows the state of the circuit when Switch is Open and Closed respectively.

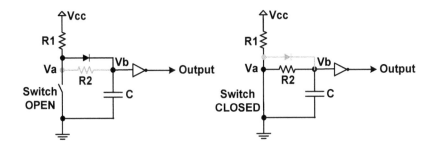

Figure 6-10: Robust RC De-bouncer states (Switch OPEN/CLOSE position)

When the Switch is OPEN, capacitor C will charge via R1 and Diode. In time, capacitor will charge and V_b will reach within 0.7V of V_{cc}. Therefore the output of the inverting schmitt tigger will be at logic 0.

When the Switch is CLOSED, the Capacitor will discharge via R2. In time capacitor C will discharge and V_b will reach 0V. Therefore the output of the inverting Schmitt trigger will be logic 1.

If bounce occurs and there are short periods of switch closure or opening, the capacitor will stop the voltage at V_b immediately reaching V_{cc} or GND. Although, bouncing will cause slight charging and discharging of the capacitor, the hysteresis of the Schmitt trigger input will stop the output from switching.

Also note that the resistor *R2* is required as a discharge path for the capacitor, without it, Capacitor will be shorted when the switch is closed. Without the diode, both *R1* and *R2* would form the capacitor charge path when the switch is open. The combination of *R1* and *R2* would increase the capacitor charge time, slowing down the circuit. Other alternative is to make the R1 smaller but this will result in unwanted waste current when the switch is closed and R1 is connected across the supply rails

6.4.2 Hardware De-bouncers

Another hardware approach is shown in Figure 6-11. It uses a cross-coupled latch made from a pair of NAND gates. This can also be designed using SR flip flop. The advantage of using a latch is that it provides a clean de-bounce without a delay limitation and will respond as fast as the contacts can open and/or close. Note that the circuit requires both normally open and normally closed contacts. In a switch, that arrangement is called "double throw". In a relay, that arrangement is called "Form C".

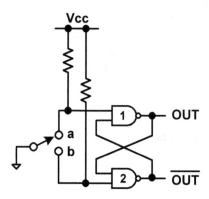

Figure 6-11: SR De-bouncer

With the switch in position "a", output of gate "1" will be Logic HIGH, regardless of value of other input. This will pull the output of the gate "2" to be held at Logic LOW. If the switch now moves between contacts and is for a while suspended in the neither region between terminals, the latch maintains its state because of the looped back zero from the gate "2". Thus, latch output is guaranteed bounce-free.

An alternative software approach to the above idea would be to run the two contacts with pull-ups directly to the input pins of the CPU. Of course CPU would observe lot of bounces but by writing a trivial code that detects any assertion of either contact, the same can be eliminated.

6.4.3 Software De-bouncing

De-bouncing a switch in software can be pretty simple though choice of algorithm may depend on application and how switches are handled. It is important to understand the problem before jumping to software techniques to de-bounce a switch.

It is important to examine the dynamic characteristics of switches and assess their environmental influences. All switches demonstrate a switch-contact bouncing action as the switch opens or closes. As mentioned before, the switch contacts actually bounce off each other several times before the contacts settle into their final position. (If the switch position is sensitive to touch, a person could cause bouncing by inadvertently touching the switch. Switch manufacturers call this inadvertent touching "playing" with the switch). These environmental interferences may include vibrations or most importantly EMI (Electromagnetic Interference).

EMI is an unwanted disturbance that affects an electrical circuit due to electromagnetic radiation emitted from an external source. This disturbance may induce noise in the switch thus causing bounces. EMI can be fixed by decent de-bounce routine.

Mentioned below are some of the techniques to de-bounce a switch in software (or firmware).

Solution A: *Read the Switch after sufficient time allowing the bounces to settle down*

A simple solution to de-bounce a switch would be to read the switch every 400-500 ms and set a status flag indicating switch state. Looking at the switch characteristics any decent switch should settle down within this time so effect of bounces would be eliminated giving a clean output every 500 msec. The only downside with this approach is slow response time. This approach would fail if user desires to operate the switch at a rate much faster than 500 ms but for all practical conditions, this should work for most of the cases.

Though a simple approach, the above technique does not provide any EMI protection. This reduces most of the random noise spikes by providing sufficient time (500 ms) for the switch to settle down to its stable state but a single glitch during that period (time when the switch status is being read) might be mistaken as a contact transition. To avoid this, software needs to be modified to read the input a couple of times each pass through the 500 ms loop and look for a stable signal. This would reject most of the EMI.

Solution B: *Interrupt the CPU on switch activation and de-bounce in ISR.*

Usually, the switch or relay connected to the computer will generate an interrupt when the contacts are activated. The interrupt will cause a subroutine (interrupt service routine) to be called. A typical de-bounce routine is given below in a sort of generic assembly language.

```
DR:         PUSH    PSW     ;   SAVE PROGRAM STATUS WORD
LOOP:       CALL    DELAY   ;   WAIT A FIXED TIME PERIOD
            IN      SWITCH  ;   READ SWITCH
            CMP     ACTIVE  ;   IS IT STILL ACTIVATED?
            JT      LOOP    ;   IF TRUE, JUMP BACK

            CALL    DELAY   ;
            POP     PSW     ;   RESTORE PROGRAM STATUS
            EI              ;   RE-ENABLE INTERRUPTS
            RETI            ;   RETURN BACK TO MAIN PROGRAM
```

The idea is that as soon as the switch is activated the De-bounce Routine (DR) is called. The DR calls another subroutine called DELAY which just kills time long enough to allow the contacts to stop bouncing. At that point the DR checks to see if the contacts are still activated (maybe the user kept a finger on the switch). If so, the DR waits for the contacts to clear. If the contacts are clear, DR calls DELAY one more time to allow for bounce on contact-release before finishing.

A de-bounce routine must be tuned to your application; the one above may not work for everything. Also, the programmer should be aware that switches and relays can lose some of their springiness as they age. That can cause the time it takes for contacts to stop bouncing to increase with time. So, the de-bounce code that worked fine when the keyboard was new might not work a year or two later. Consult the switch manufacturer for data on worst-case bounce times.

Solution C: *Use a Counter to eliminate the noise and validate switch state*

Another idea would be to make a counter count up as long as the signal is Low, and reset this counter when the signal is High. If the counter reaches a certain fixed value, which should be 1 or 2 times bigger noise pulses, this means that the current pulse is a valid pulse.

Snapshot of a sample C code is shown below.

```
// include files
unsigned char counter; // Variable used to count
unsigned char T_valid; // Variable used as the minimum
                       // duration of a valid pulse

void main(){
    P1 = 255;          // Initialize port 1 as input port
    T_valid = 100;     // Arbitrary number from 0 to 255 where
                       // the pulse if validated
    while(1){                  // infinite loop
        if (counter < 255){ // prevent the counter to roll
                            // back to 0
            counter++;
        }
        if (P1_0 == 1){
            counter = 0; // reset the counter back to 0
        }
        if (counter > T_valid){
            //....
            // Code to be executed when a valid
            // pulse is detected.
            //....
        }

        //....
        // Rest of you program goes here.
        //....
    }
}
```

6.4.4 De-bouncing Guidelines

A variety of de-bouncing approach have been discussed in previous section, however it is not a good idea to consume lot of CPU cycles to resolve a bounce. De-bounce is a small problem and deserves a small part of the computer's attention so one should choose an approach that minimizes CPU overhead. Below are some of the guidelines that should be followed to have robust de-bouncing mechanism in a circuit:

- CPU overhead associated with de-bouncing should be minimized.
- The un-debounced switch must connect to a programmed I/O pin, never to an interrupt of the CPU. If done, this may result in

multiple interrupts due to bouncing. Also this increases the load on CPU as it would go to execute ISR with every interrupt.

- A delay in an ISR cannot be tolerated, stick to the fact that ISRs have to be quick. The interrupt associated with the switch state should not be used a clock or data signal of a flip-flop as this may violate minimum clock width or the data setup and hold time

- Switch input should not be sampled at a rate synchronous to the events in the outside world that might create periodic EMI. Sampling at common frequencies like 50/60 Hz should be avoided. Even mechanical vibration can create periodic interference. For Automobiles, even sampling at a rate synchronous to engine vibration or vibration of a steering column may induce EMI.

- System should respond instantly to the switch (user) input. In case the status of the switch gets indicated to the LED or display; user may want to do that quickly to avoid any confusion as to what is seen on the display or LED.

- Instead of having a delay (in milliseconds or seconds) to wait for input to get stable, use a timer to interrupt the CPU at regular interval (say every few milliseconds). This keeps the de-bouncing code portable when porting to a new compiler or CPU rather than changing the wait states every time clock rate changes or CPU changes.

6.4.5 De-bouncing on Multiple Inputs

For all practical reasons, a system may have multiple banks of switches. While it is seen how a single input switch can be de-bounced it does not make sense to de-bounce multiple inputs individually when all input switches can be handled at once with little overhead on the CPU. This section extends the technique or de-bouncing algorithm to handle multiple switches or inputs. Figure 6-12 shows a system with multiple input switches.

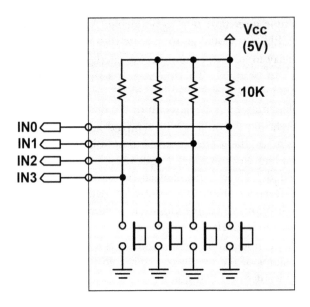

Figure 6-12: Circuit with multiple Switches

De-bouncing Algorithm (pseudo code) to handle multiple inputs is shown below:

```
// This program demonstrates the simultaneous debouncing
// of multiple inputs. The input subroutine is easily
// adjusted to handle any number of inputs

Main:
GOSUB Debounce_Switches // get debounced inputs
PAUSE 50                 // time between readings
GOTO Main                // Continue the loop
END

Debounce_Switches:
switches = 0xF           // enable all four inputs
FOR x = 1 TO 10
   switches = switches & ~Switch_Inputs // test inputs
   PAUSE 5               // delay between tests
NEXT
RETURN
```

The purpose of *Debounce_Switches* subroutine is to make sure that the inputs stay on solid for 50 milliseconds with no contact bouncing. De-bounced inputs will be retuned in the variable, *switches*, with a valid input represented by a 1 in the switch position.

The *Debounce_Switches* routine starts by assuming that all switch inputs will be valid, so all the bits of switches are set to one. Then, the inputs are scanned and compared to the previous state in *FOR-NEXT* loop. Since the inputs are active low (zero when pressed), the one's compliment operator inverts them. The *And* operator (&) is used to update the current state. For a switch to be valid, it must remain pressed through the entire *FOR-NEXT* loop.

Here's how the de-bouncing technique works: When a switch is pressed, the input to the switch will be zero as shown in Figure 12. The one's compliment operator will invert zero to one. One "ANDed" with one is still one, so that switch remains valid. If the switch is not pressed, the input to the switch will be one (because of the 10K pull-up to V_{dd}). One is inverted to zero. Zero "ANDed" with any number is zero and will cause the switch to remain invalid through the entire de-bounce cycle.

Rather than having a fixed delay of 50 millseconds between de-bounced inputs, it is always recommended to trigger the *Debounce_Switches* routine by timer interrupt that makes the design portable.

6.5 Existing Solutions

For the designs that do not include de-bounce circuitry on external inputs, system may choose to use external de-bounce ICs. From the more popular ones, MAXIM MAX6816/MAX6817/MAX6818 series offer single, dual, and octal switch de-bouncers that provide clean interfacing of mechanical switches to digital systems. Figure 6-13 shows show interconnection of MAX6816 to any Microprocessor or chip that needs to de-bounce input pin but does not include internal de-bounce circuitry.

MAX681x series accept one or more bouncing inputs from a mechanical switch and produce a clean digital output after a short, preset qualification delay.

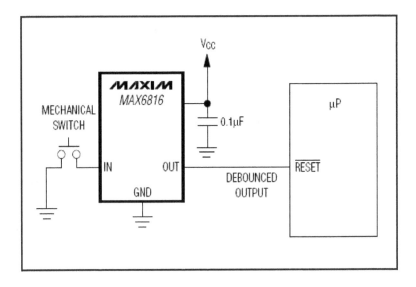

Figure 6-13: De-bounce RESET input with MAX6816[7] [21]

The MAX6818 octal switch de-bouncer is designed for data-bus interfacing. The MAX6818 monitors switches and provides a switch change-of-state output (CH), simplifying microprocessor (μP) polling and interrupts.

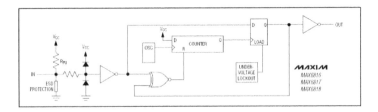

Figure 6-14: MAX6816/6817/6818 Block Diagram[7] [22]

Virtually all mechanical switches bounce upon opening or closing. These switch de-bouncers remove bounce when a switch opens or closes by requiring that sequentially clocked inputs remain in the same state for a

---

[7] Copyright Maxim Integrated Products (http://maxim-ic.com). Used by Permission

number of sampling periods. The output does not change until the input is stable for duration of 40 ms.

Figure 6-14 shows the functional blocks consisting of an on-chip oscillator, counter, exclusive-NOR gate, and D flip-flop. When the input does not equal the output, the XNOR gate issues a counter reset. When the switch input state is stable for the full qualification period, the counter clocks the flip-flop, updating the output.

The under-voltage lockout circuitry ensures that the outputs are at the correct state on power-up. While the supply voltage is below the under-voltage threshold, the de-bounce circuitry remains transparent. Switch states are present at the logic outputs without delay.

Apart from the de-bounce circuitry, above Maxim devices includes ±15kV ESD-protection on all pins to protect against electrostatic discharges encountered during handling and assembly.

7. Power Management

7.1 Introduction

Today's designs require an increasing number of power rails and supply solutions in System-on-chip , with loads ranging from a few uA for standby supplies to over 100s of mA voltage regulators. It is important to choose the appropriate solution for the targeted application and to meet specified performance requirements, such as high efficiency, tight printed circuit board (PCB) space, accurate output regulation, fast transient response, low solution cost, etc. Power management design is becoming a more frequent and challenging task for system designers, many of who may not have strong power backgrounds.

The chapter is aimed at system engineers who may not be very familiar with power supply designs and selection. The basic operating principles of linear regulators and SMPS are explained and the advantages and disadvantages of each solution are discussed. Chapter expands to include power supply design models and considerations for embedded systems to provide most optimal solution for the target application based on power targets, efficiency and area tradeoff.

7.2 Need for Linear Regulator

A power converter generates output voltage and current for the load from a given input power source. It needs to meet the load voltage or current regulation requirement during steady-state and transient conditions. It also must protect the load and system in case of a component failure.

Let's start with a simple example. Let's say in an embedded system, a 12V bus rail is available from the front-end power supply. On the system board, a 3.3V voltage is needed to power an operational amplifier (op amp). The simplest approach to generate the 3.3V is to use a resistor divider from the 12V bus, as shown in Figure 7-1. Does it work well? The answer is usually "*No*". The op amp's V_{CC} pin current may vary under different operating conditions. If a fixed resistor divider is used, the chip V_{CC} voltage varies with load. Besides, the 12V bus input may not be well regulated. There may be many other loads in the same system sharing the 12V rail. Because of the bus impedance, the 12V bus voltage varies with the bus loading conditions. As a result, a resistor divider cannot provide a regulated 3.3V to the op amp to ensure its proper operation. Therefore, a dedicated voltage regulation loop is needed.

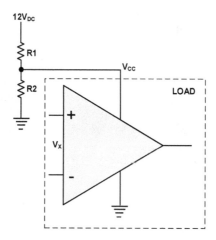

Figure 7-1: Resistor Divider Generates 3.3V$_{DC}$ from 12V Bus Input

As shown in Figure 7-2, the feedback loop needs to adjust the top resistor R1 value to dynamically regulate the 3.3V on V$_{CC}$.

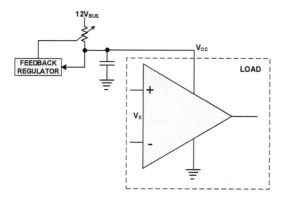

Figure 7-2: Feedback Loop Adjusts Series Resistor R1 Value to Regulate 3.3V [23]

This kind of variable resistor can be implemented with a linear regulator, as shown in Figure 7-3. A linear regulator operates a bipolar or field effect power transistor (FET) in its linear mode. So the transistor works as a variable resistor in series with the output load. To establish the feedback loop, conceptually, an error amplifier senses the DC output voltage via a sampling resistor network R_A and R_B, and then compares the feedback voltage V_{FB} with a reference voltage V_{REF}. The error amplifier output voltage drives the base of the series power transistor via a current amplifier. When either the input V_{BUS} voltage decreases or the load current increases, the V_{CC} output voltage goes down. The feedback voltage V_{FB} decreases as well. As a result, the feedback error amplifier and current amplifier generate more current into the base of the transistor Q1. This reduces the voltage drop V_{CE} and hence brings back the V_{CC} output voltage, so that V_{FB} equals V_{REF}. On the other hand, if the V_{CC} output voltage goes up, in a similar way, the negative feedback circuit increases V_{CE} to ensure the accurate regulation of the 3.3V output. In summary, any variation of V_O is absorbed by the linear regulator transistor's V_{CE} voltage. So the output voltage V_{CC} is always constant and well regulated.

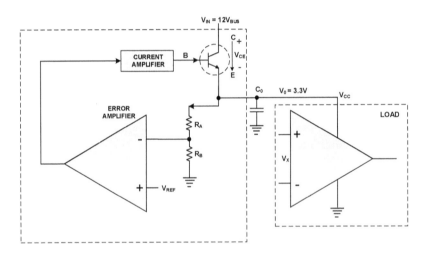

Figure 7-3: A Linear Regulator Implements a Variable Resistor to Regulate Output Voltage [23]

7.3 Linear Regulator Efficiency

A major drawback of using linear regulators can be the excessive power dissipation of its series transistor Q1 operating in a linear mode. As explained previously, a linear regulator transistor is conceptually a variable resistor. Since all the load current must pass through the series transistor, its power dissipation is $P_{LOSS} = (V_{IN} - V_O) \times I_O$. In this case, the efficiency of a linear regulator can be quickly estimated by:

$$\eta = \frac{P_{OUT}}{P_{OUT} + P_{LOSS}} = \frac{V_O \times I_O}{V_O \times I_O + (V_{IN} - V_O) \times I_O} = \frac{V_O}{V_{IN}}$$

So in the Table 1-1 example, when the input is 12V and output is 3.3V, the linear regulator efficiency is just 27.5%. In this case, 82.5% of the input power is just wasted and generates heat in the regulator. This means that the transistor must have the thermal capability to handle its power/heat dissipation at worst case at maximum V_{IN} and full load. So the size of the linear regulator and its heat sink may be large, especially when V_O is much less than V_{IN}.

7.4 Low Dropout Regulator (LDO)

The linear regulator can be very efficient if V_O is close to V_{IN}. However, the linear regulator has another limitation, which is the minimum voltage difference between V_{IN} and V_O. The transistor in the Linear Regulator must be operated in its linear mode. So it requires a certain minimum voltage drop across the collector to emitter of a bipolar transistor or drain to source of a FET. When V_O is too close to V_{IN}, the Linear Regulator may be unable to regulate output voltage anymore. The linear regulators that can work with low headroom ($V_{IN} - V_O$) are called low dropout regulators (LDOs).

It is also clear that a linear regulator or an LDO can only provide step-down DC/DC conversion. In applications that require V_O voltage to be higher than V_{IN} voltage, or need negative V_O voltage from a positive V_{IN} voltage, linear regulators obviously do not work.

7.5 Benefits of Linear Regulator

There are many applications in which linear regulators or LDOs provide superior solutions to switching supplies, including:

- **Simple/low cost solutions**. Linear regulator or LDO solutions are simple and easy to use, especially for low power applications with low output current where thermal stress is not critical. No external power inductor is required.

- **Low noise/low ripple applications**: For noise-sensitive applications, such as communication and radio devices, minimizing the supply noise is very critical. Linear regulators have very low output voltage ripple because there are no elements switching on and off frequently and linear regulators can have very high bandwidth. So there is little EMI problem. SMPS generally have higher noise level or output ripple compared to linear regulators/LDOs.

- **Fast Transient applications:** The linear regulator feedback loop is usually internal, so no external compensation is required. Typically, linear regulators have wider control loop bandwidth and faster transient response than that of SMPS, which makes them ideal for a fast boot applications.

- **Low dropout applications:** For applications where output voltage is close to the input voltage, LDOs may be more efficient than an SMPS. Because there is no AC switching loss in an LR, the light load efficiency of an LR or an LDO is similar to its full load efficiency. An SMPS usually has lower light load efficiency because of its AC switching losses. In battery powered applications in which light load efficiency is also critical, an LDO can provide a better solution than an SMPS.

In summary, designers use linear regulators or LDOs because they are simple, low noise, low cost, easy to use and provide fast transient response. If V_O is close to V_{IN}, an LDO may be more efficient than an SMPS.

7.6 Switch Mode Power Supply (SMPS)

Though there are many benefits of using Linear regular or LDO, they are highly inefficient for higher current loads, especially for the cases where difference between the input and output voltage is significant.

In a Switch Mode Power Supply (SMPS), the transistors are operating in switching mode instead of linear mode. This indicates that when the transistor is on and conducting current, the voltage drop across its power path is minimal. When the transistor is off and blocking high voltage, there is almost no current through its power path. So the semiconductor transistor works like an ideal switch. Since pass transistor spends very little time in the high dissipation transitions, the power loss in the transistor is therefore minimized.

Switching regulators are used as replacements for linear regulators when higher efficiency, smaller size or lighter weight is required, especially in high current applications.

Unlike a linear regulator that provides the desired output voltage by dissipating excess power in ohmic losses as explained in previous section, a switched-mode power supply regulates either output voltage or current by switching ideal storage elements, like inductors and capacitors, into and out of different electrical configurations. Ideal switching elements (e.g., transistors operated outside of their active mode) have no resistance when "*closed*" and carry no current when "*open*", and so the converters can theoretically operate with 100% efficiency (i.e., all input power is delivered to the load; no power is wasted as dissipated heat).

Unlike linear regulators, which can only step down an input, SMPS are attractive because a topology can be selected to fit nearly any output voltage.

7.6.1 SMPS Topologies: Selecting the Right Switching Regulator

Manufacturers sell different types of switching regulators. The location of the storage elements in reference to the switching elements and their quantities generally determines the type of switching supply configuration, as can be seen in various architectures.

a) Buck Converter

In the generic buck configuration, the switch controls the current flowing into the inductor. The inductor stores the energy for the load.

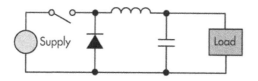

Figure 7-4: Buck Configuration for a switching regulator

Buck Converter is known as the step-down converter and is the most commonly used switching converter (Figure 7-4). It's used to down-convert a DC voltage to a lower DC voltage of the same polarity. Although linear regulators can also perform this function, switching buck regulators can do it with higher efficiency.

b) Boost Converter

The generic boost configuration steps up the voltage since the inductor is placed prior to the switch.

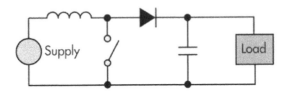

Figure 7-5: Boost Configuration of a Switching Regulator

The boost converter, also known as the step-up converter, takes a DC input voltage and produces a DC output voltage that's higher in value than the input but of the same polarity (Figure 7-5). Linear regulators cannot provide this feature.

c) Buck-Boost Converter

The generic buck-boost configuration can output a voltage that is either greater or less than the input voltage magnitude, including negative voltages.

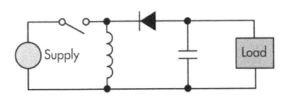

Figure 7-6: Buck-Boost Configuration of a Switching Regulator

The buck-boost or inverting regulator produces a DC voltage that is above, below, or opposite in polarity to the input (Figure 7-6). The negative output voltage can be larger or smaller than the input voltage. There's usually a limitation in the $V_{IN} - (-V_{OUT})$ magnitude that the regulator can handle. Buck-boost can work with input voltages above and below the output.

d) Single Ended Primary Inductor Converter (SEPIC)

The single-ended primary-inductor converter (SEPIC) is similar to a traditional buck-boost converter (Figure 7-7). The voltage output can be greater than, less than, or equal to that at its input. The duty cycle of the control transistor controls its output. The SEPIC also is capable of true shutdown. When the switch is turned off, its output drops to 0 V.

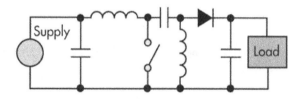

Figure 7-7: SEPIC Configuration

e) CUK Converter

The generic CUK configuration can output a voltage that is either greater or less than the input voltage magnitude.

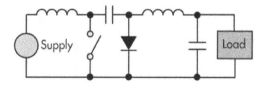

Figure 7-8: CUK Converter

The CUK converter's output voltage can be greater than or less than the input voltage magnitude (Figure 7-8). It uses a capacitor as its main energy-storage component. By using inductors on the input and output, the CUK converter produces very little input and output current ripple. And, it has minimized electromagnetic interference (EMI) radiation.

f) Switched Capacitor Converter

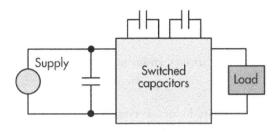

Figure 7-9: Switched Capacitor Regulator

Also known as a charge pump, the switched capacitor regulator uses capacitors as energy storage elements to create a higher or lower voltage (Figure 7-9). It can generate arbitrary voltages, depending on the controller and circuit topology. Charge pumps can double, triple, halve, invert, or fractionally multiply or scale voltages such as x3/2, x4/3, and x2/3. It also can provide multiple outputs.

g) Flyback Converter

The flyback converter is the most versatile of all the topologies (Figure 7-10). It allows for one or more output voltages, some of which may be opposite in polarity. Additionally, it is very popular in battery-powered systems. It provides isolation as well.

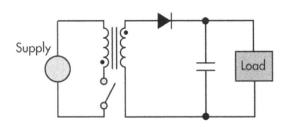

Figure 7-10: Flyback configuration

The generic flyback configuration is similar to a buck-boost converter with the inductor replaced by a transformer. The energy is temporarily stored in a magnetic field in the inductor air gap before it is transferred to the secondary side.

h) Forward Converter

The forward converter is a buck regulator with a transformer inserted between the buck switch and the load (Figure 7-11). It provides both higher and lower voltage outputs as well as isolation. It also might be more energy efficient than a flyback converter [24].

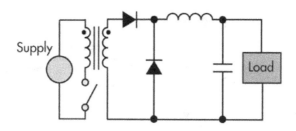

Figure 7-11: Forward Converter

In the generic forward configuration, the energy is transferred directly between the primary and secondary sides.

i) Push-Pull Converter

The push-pull converter is a forward converter with two primaries (Figure 7-12). It can generate multiple output voltages, some of which may be negative in polarity. It provides isolation as well. However, it requires very good matching of the switch transistors to prevent unequal ON times [24].

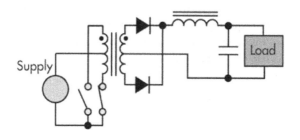

Figure 7-12: Push-Pull Converter

The pairs of switches (transistors) in a generic symmetrical push-pull circuit help to maintain a steadier input current and create less noise on the input line.

j) Half-Bridge Converter

The half-bridge converter is usually operated directly from the AC line (Figure 7-13). The switch transistor drive circuitry must be isolated from the transistors, requiring the use of base drive transformers [24].

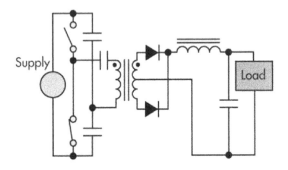

Figure 7-13: Half-Bridge Converter

The primary-side capacitors in a generic half-bridge configuration are used to produce a constant half voltage at their junction, reducing the stress on the switches to only the input voltage.

k) Full-Bridge Converter

The full-bridge converter provides isolation from the AC line (Figure 7-14). The pulse-width modulation (PWM) control circuitry is referenced to the output ground, requiring a dedicated voltage rail to run the control circuits. The base drive voltages for the switch transistors have to be transformer-coupled because of the required isolation [24].

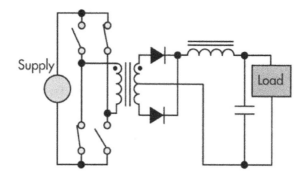

Figure 7-14: Full-Bridge Converter

Only the diagonal switches in the generic full-bridge configuration are switched ON simultaneously. This provides full input voltage across the primary winding of the transformer. The polarity of the transformer reverses in each half cycle.

7.6.2 SMPS Topologies and Conversion Theory

As mentioned in the previous section, SMPSs can convert a DC input voltage into a different DC output voltage, depending on the circuit topology. While there are numerous SMPS topologies used in the engineering world, three are fundamental and seen most often. These topologies (Figure 7-15) are classified according to their conversion function:

- Step-down Converter (Buck)
- Step-up Converter (Boost)
- Step-up/down Converter (Buck-Boost or inverter).

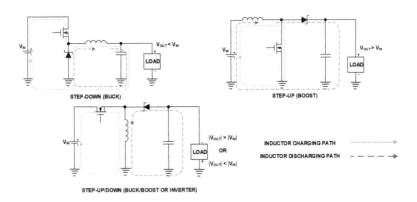

Figure 7-15: Buck, Boost, and Buck-Boost compose the fundamental SMPS topologies[8] [21]

All three fundamental topologies include a MOSFET switch, a diode, an output capacitor, and an inductor. The MOSFET, which is the actively controlled component in the circuit, is interfaced to a controller (not shown). This controller applies a pulse-width-modulated (PWM) square-wave signal to the MOSFET's gate, thereby switching the device on and off. To maintain a constant output voltage, the controller senses the SMPS output voltage and varies the duty cycle (D) of the square-wave signal, dictating how long the MOSFET is on during each switching period (T_S). The value of D, which is the ratio of the square wave's on time to its switching period (T_{ON}/T_S), directly affects the voltage observed at the SMPS output. This relationship is illustrated in equations 4 and 5.

The on and off states of the MOSFET divide the SMPS circuit into two phases: a charge phase and a discharge phase, both of which describe the energy transfer of the inductor (see the path loops in Figure 7-15). Energy stored in the inductor during the charging phase is transferred to the output load and capacitor during the discharge phase. The capacitor supports the load while the inductor is charging and sustains the output voltage. This cyclical transfer of energy between the circuit elements maintains the output voltage at the proper value, in accordance with its topology.

The inductor is central to the energy transfer from source to load during each switching cycle. Without it, the SMPS would not function when the MOSFET is switched. The energy (E) stored in an inductor (L) is dependent upon its current (I):

$$E = \frac{1}{2} \times L \times I^2 \tag{1}$$

Therefore, energy change in the inductor is gauged by the change in its current (ΔI_L), which is due to the voltage applied across it (V_L) over a specific time period (ΔT):

$$\Delta I_L = \frac{V_L \times \Delta T}{L} \tag{2}$$

The (ΔI_L) is a linear ramp, as a constant voltage is applied across the inductor during each switching phase (Figure 7-16). The inductor voltage during the switching phase can be determined by performing a Kirchhoff's voltage loop, paying careful attention to polarities and V_{IN}/V_{OUT} relationships. For example, inductor voltage for the step-up converter during the discharge phase is - (V_{OUT} - V_{IN}). Because $V_{OUT} > V_{IN}$, the inductor voltage is negative.

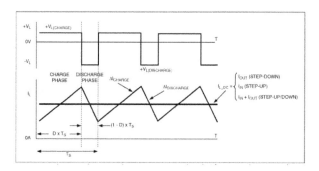

Figure 7-16: Voltage and Current Characteristics are detailed for a steady-state inductor[9] [21]

---

[9] Copyright Maxim Integrated Products (http://maxim-ic.com). Used by Permission

During the charge phase, the MOSFET is on, the diode is reverse biased, and energy is transferred from the voltage source to the inductor (Figure 7-15). Inductor current ramps up because V_L is positive. Also, the output capacitance transfers the energy it stored from the previous cycle to the load in order to maintain a constant output voltage. During the discharge phase, the MOSFET turns off, and the diode becomes forward biased and, therefore, conducts. Because the source is no longer charging the inductor, the inductor's terminals swap polarity as it discharges energy to the load and replenishes the output capacitor (Figure 7-15). The inductor current ramps down as it imparts energy, according to the same transfer relationship given previously.

The charge/discharge cycles repeat and maintain a steady-state switching condition. During the circuit's progression to a steady state, inductor current builds up to its final level, which is a superposition of DC current and the ramped AC current (or inductor ripple current) developed during the two circuit phases (Figure 7-16). The DC current level is related to output current, but depends on the position of the inductor in the SMPS circuit.

The ripple current must be filtered out by the SMPS in order to deliver true DC current to the output. This filtering action is accomplished by the output capacitor, which offers little opposition to the high-frequency AC current. The unwanted output-ripple current passes through the output capacitor, and maintains the capacitor's charge as the current passes to ground. Thus, the output capacitor also stabilizes the output voltage. In non-ideal applications, however, equivalent series resistance (ESR) of the output capacitor causes output-voltage ripple proportional to the ripple current that flows through it.

So, in summary, energy is shuttled between the source, the inductor, and the output capacitor to maintain a constant output voltage and to supply the load. But, how does the SMPS's energy transfer determine its output voltage-conversion ratio? This ratio is easily calculated when steady state is understood as it applies to periodic waveforms.

To be in a steady state, a variable that repeats with period T_S must be equal at the beginning and end of each period. Because inductor current is periodic due to the charge and discharge phases described previously, the inductor current at the beginning of the PWM period must equal inductor current at the end. This means that the change in inductor current during the charge phase (ΔI_{CHARGE}) must equal the change in inductor current during the discharge phase ($\Delta I_{DISCHARGE}$). Equating the change in inductor current for the charge and discharge phases, an interesting result is achieved, which is also referred to as the volt-second rule:

$$|\Delta I_{CHARGE}| = |\Delta I_{DISCHARGE}|$$

$$\left|\frac{V_{L(CHARGE)} \times D \times T_S}{L}\right| = \left|\frac{V_{L(DISCHARGE)} \times (1-D) \times T_S}{L}\right| \tag{3}$$

$$\left|V_{L(CHARGE)}\right| \times D \times T_S = \left|V_{L(DISCHARGE)}\right| \times (1-D) \times T_S$$

Simply put, the inductor voltage-time product during each circuit phase is equal. This means that, by observing the SMPS circuits of Figure 7-15, the ideal steady-state voltage-/current-conversion ratios can be found with little effort. For the step-down circuit, a Kirchhoff's voltage loop around the charge phase circuit reveals that inductor voltage is the difference between V_{IN} and V_{OUT}. Likewise, inductor voltage during the discharge phase circuit is -V_{OUT}. Using the volt-second rule from equation 3, the following voltage-conversion ratio is determined:

$$|V_{IN} - V_{OUT}| \times D = |-V_{OUT}| \times (1-D)$$

$$\frac{V_{OUT}}{V_{IN}} = D \tag{4}$$

Further, input power (P_{IN}) equals output power (P_{OUT}) in an ideal circuit. Thus, the current-conversion ratio is found:

$$P_{IN} = P_{OUT}$$

$$I_{IN} \times V_{IN} = I_{OUT} \times V_{OUT}$$

$$\frac{I_{IN}}{I_{OUT}} = \frac{V_{OUT}}{V_{IN}} = D$$

From these results, it is seen that the step-down converter reduces V_{IN} by a factor of D, while input current is a D-multiple of load current. Table 7-1 lists the conversion ratios for the topologies depicted in Figure 7-15.

Topology	Voltage-Conversion Ratio	Current-Conversion Ratio
Step-Down	$\dfrac{V_{OUT}}{V_{IN}} = D$	$\dfrac{I_{IN}}{I_{OUT}} = D$
Step-Up	$\dfrac{V_{OUT}}{V_{IN}} = \dfrac{1}{1-D}$	$\dfrac{I_{IN}}{I_{OUT}} = \dfrac{1}{1-D}$
Step-Up/Down	$\dfrac{V_{OUT}}{V_{IN}} = \dfrac{D}{1-D}$	$\dfrac{I_{IN}}{I_{OUT}} = \dfrac{D}{1-D}$

Table 7-1: SMPS Conversion Ratios

Generally, all SMPS conversion ratios can be found with the method used to solve equations 3 and 5, though complex topologies can be more difficult to analyze.

7.7 Power Supply Design Models

An embedded system could be powered in any one of the following models:

- Wall powered
- Wall powered with battery backup
- Primarily Battery backed up
- Fully powered battery

Wall Powered Devices:

These devices operate fully on power supply available from wall power. They typically consume more power and work in tandem with systems that consumes a lot of power, that they are redundant when the underlying system could not be powered on. Many of the devices in use fall under this category including medical devices, industrial systems etc.

Wall Powered with Battery Backup:

These classes of devices are very similar to above case but will have a limited power backup using batteries. This backup is useful to properly shutdown the system and to store the system configuration and acquired values safely till full power is back.

Primarily Battery Backed up:

The most common example of these devices is mobile phones. They are designed to work primarily with battery power supply. Whenever needed the system can be charged back. It incorporates a full-fledged battery charging and managing circuitry.

Fully Battery Powered:

These devices are designed to work only from battery supply that does not have a charging mechanism. These batteries have to be externally charged or non-rechargeable batteries like a coin-cell.

Apart from these, there are many power sources being used in embedded systems including photo-voltaic – solar power, etc. With the upcoming wearable computing becoming a trend, the power supplies include generating from unconventional sources like audio jack of smart phone, human/mechanical movements or even body heat etc.

7.8 Power Supply Design Considerations

7.8.1 Wall Powered Systems

Figure 7-17 typically explains the power supply design for wall power with battery backup devices.

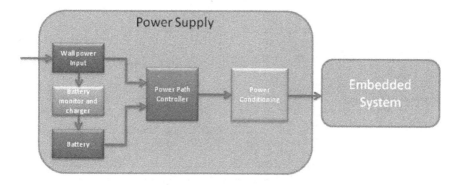

Figure 7-17: Wall Powered Embedded Systems [25]

The DC power input from the wall socket is used to power the system. If the wall power is absent, the battery powers the system. The Power path controller is used to route the power from preferable source. The power conditioning circuit finally supplies to the load at the required voltage and current. Battery monitoring and charger circuit is necessary for managing the battery.

Wall power is obtained from AC wall adapter plugged in the wall socket. It provides constant low voltage DC suitable for running the system from the high level AC source in the wall socket. The main factors to be considered on selecting the wall power are voltage and current. The voltage supplied by the wall power should be more enough to satisfy the input voltage requirement of the power conditioning circuit usually comprising of linear or SMPS regulators. Also if the power supply system incorporates battery charging, then the voltage requirement of the battery charger should be taken into account.

Power Supply for these systems are usually big and integrated separately instead of being part of the embedded system SoC. One good example is laptop battery.

7.8.2 Battery Powered Systems

Battery powered systems can cover a wide range of embedded systems all the way from low-end systems that takes very low current running bare metal operating system or RTOS to all the way to higher end system running sophisticated multimedia and operating system like Linux.

System Type	Type of Input	System Load	Operation System
Ultra Low Power	Single Supply	<50-70 mA	Bare Metal, RTOS
Low-End	Single/Multiple Supply	< 100-150mA	Bare Metal, RTOS
Mid-end	Multiple Supply	150-250 mA	RTOS, Linux, Android wear,
High-end	Multiple Supply	> 250 mA	Linux, Android wear

Table 7-2: Battery Power embedded systems

  a) *Ultra Low Power Embedded Systems*

This is applicable to small embedded devices that generally run on single supply voltage. Generally for lower end embedded system, this would normally be 3.0-3.3V input supply. The external power supply is then regulated by series on internal regulator to generate different voltage for different power domains. Figure 7-18 shows an example with 3.3V input supply that is internally regulated to generated 1.8V and 1.2V.

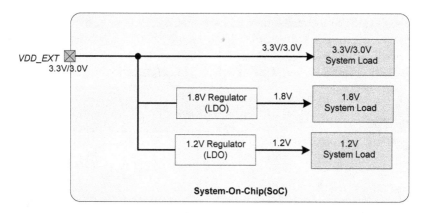

Figure 7-18: Single Supply Embedded Systems

Another option for 1.2V regulator could be to cascade it with 1.8V regulator where 1.2V regulator is based on output of 1.8V regulator as shown in Figure 7-19. Overall efficiency of regulation system may still be same as original scheme due to efficiency loss in 1.8V regulator and 1.2V regulator; however depending on the available devices it may be easier to design regulator that converts from 1.8V input instead of 3V input, however this may not be always true, based on available technology restrictions.

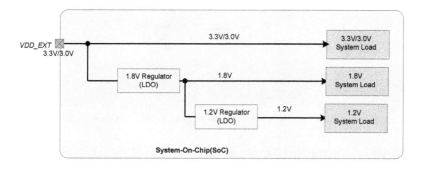

Figure 7-19: Single Supply Embedded Systems with cascaded regulators

This type of scheme is very well suited for low-end microcontrollers where main requirements are low power and cost and where system load on each rail is low such that efficiency loss due to regulator is not really a consideration.

Common source for single 3.0/3.V supply could be external 3.3V regulator.

Sub-set of the use-cases may include scenarios where complete system is powered from a USB cable (5V). Figure 7-20 shows the case where Microcontroller includes 5V to 3.3V on-chip USB regulator while Figure 7-21 the scenario where USB regulator is kept outside the microcontroller.

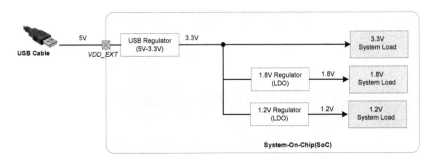

Figure 7-20: Single Supply USB Powered regulation with on-chip USB regulator

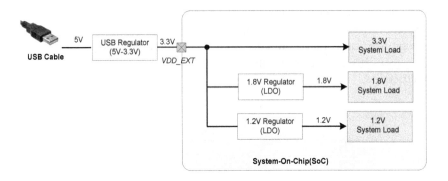

Figure 7-21: Single Supply USB Powered regulation with external USB regulator

For highly integrated system where cost and small form factor is highest priority, there are specific advantages to integrate USB regulator on-chip, however both USB cases are limited by the amount of current that can be sourced from USB cable.

b) Low-end Embedded Systems

These systems have higher capability then *"Ultra-Low"* end embedded system with more system integration but still works on bare metal OS or RTOS. Single Supply system would still be similar to a) but with higher current load on 3.3V/5V supply.

NOTE: *When powered with USB cable, there is an absolute limit of 150 mA that can be sourced from the USB cable.*

These systems may also extend to include some sort of external volatile memory like DDR (DDR2, DDR3, LPDDR2 or Similar) that would require separate power for the DDR IOs and external DRAM Memory which needs to powered separately outside the SoC. This can be done by having another external regulator dedicated for DDR supply that also powers the external DRAM memory.

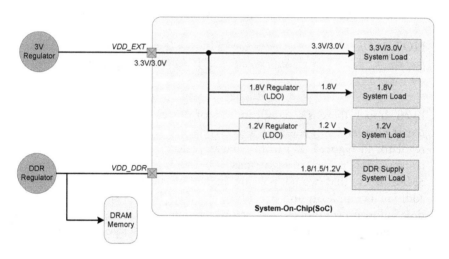

Figure 7-22: Multi-Supply embedded system with separate supply for DDR

Since there could be low power modes where DRAM is powered off while system is still powered in low power modes, it make all sense to decouple DRAM supply internally with core supply even if both requires same voltage since in this case DDR regulator can be switched off in low power modes providing lower system current. There are other better reasons to do so as well.

There may be other scenarios where embedded system is powered by 1.8V chargeable Li-Ion Battery (Figure 7-23) replacing 3.3V regulator for the cases where SoC does not require 3.3V at all.

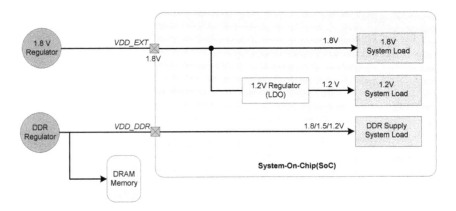

Figure 7-23: Multi-Supply system with 1.8V input supply

NOTE: *One of the common sources for 1.8V could be chargeable 1.8V Li-Ion battery (not shown), however for systems running of 1.8V battery generally would be DDR-less low power applications.*

Even though there is a significant loss of power efficiency, specifically on the regulators that generated lower voltage (for example 1.8V and 1.2V regulator in Figure 7-22) from what is available from the source, current consumption is low enough (max 100-150mA) to tradeoff inclusion of SMPS Buck that would provide higher efficiency but at the cost of additional complexity and size. Moreover if application spends most of the time in low power modes where current requirement is really limited, LDO based linear regulator is all that is required to keep design simple and cost low.

c) Mid-end Embedded Systems

These categories of embedded systems generally are more capable then "*low-end*" embedded systems, thus consuming more power due to nature of application. Some sort of display capabilities with support of full operating system like Linux would be very common. Android-wear would also fall in this category for handheld consumer type applications.

Consumer type portable applications in this category may run from chargeable Lithium-Ion battery but may not be limited to, thus higher power efficiency is very important in the active power modes. One of the ways to achieve is to include SMPS-Buck (shown as DC-DC converter) for the supply with higher load as shown in Figure 7-24.

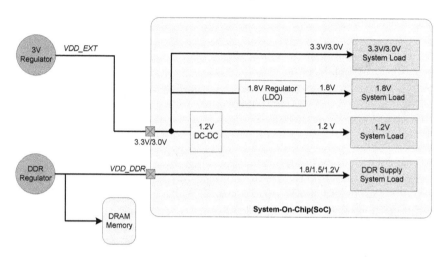

Figure 7-24: DC-DC Converter on 1.2V supply for higher power efficiency

For higher load supplies like core supply in a SoC, having SMPS-Buck would really provide much higher efficiency. If the difference in Source supply and generated supply is high, having a Linear regulator for higher loads would be very in-efficient (Figure 7-25).

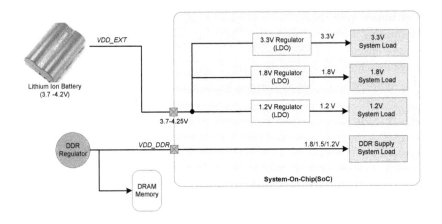

Figure 7-25: Un-recommended approach for Power efficient regulation

In this particular case, using internal linear regulator on high load supply (1.2V) would mean reduced efficiency.

$$Efficiency\ (\eta) = \frac{V_O}{V_{IN}} = \frac{1.2V}{4.25V} = 28\ \%$$

So for a 200 mA load on 1.2V supply (= 240 mW), system power from the Lithium-Ion battery would still be 4.25V x 200 mA =850mW.

For a higher efficiency system, one may consider including SMPS (DC-DC) on 1.2V supply (Figure 7-26). Main difference from what is shown in Figure 7-24 is that former is powered by 3.3V external regulator while later (Figure 7-26) is powered from Lithium Ion battery (3.7-4.2V). Since DC-DC are highly efficient (above 90%), for higher loads would provide enable lower system power thus increasing battery life.

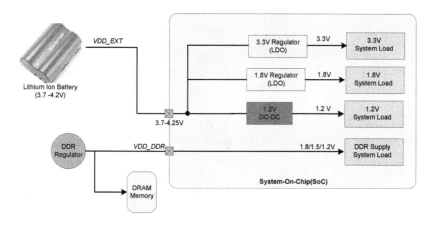

Figure 7-26: High efficiency power system with DC-DC converter

d) High-end Embedded Systems

Any embedded systems in this category that consumes higher current will generally rely on external Power management ICs (PMIC) to be able to provide different supply voltages for the SoC with the highest power efficiency.

Often all power supply may not come from PMIC based on PMIC selected and the number of output tunable supplies that are available versus what is required by the SoC. An example is shown in Figure 7-27 where 1.8V supply is not available from the PMIC and is generated internally through on-chip LDO.

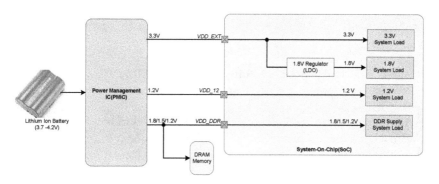

Figure 7-27: Efficiency Power system with external PMIC for high load embedded systems

This would still keep power system very efficient if the load on 1.8V LDO is "*low*". For a higher load, an internal DC-DC on that supply may be necessary (not shown).

For more complex system, there could be more scenarios where PMIC may be required to be turned off during low power modes with only part of the SoC operational. One way to efficiently do this is by having a separate regulator (separate from PMIC) that only powers the "*Always ON logic*" (Figure 7-28) that is necessary to remain enabled during low power modes, for example. This provides a best combination of low power (since PMIC remains OFF during low power modes) and fast recovery time (since standalone regulator has faster response time then PMIC) from low power modes.

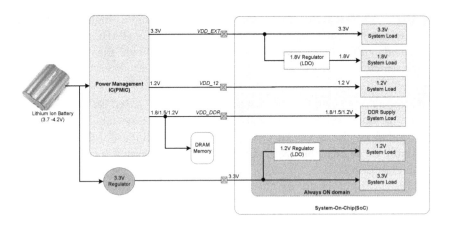

Figure 7-28: Combination of PMIC and internal LDOs for a power efficient embedded system.

Another example where this may be very useful is dual core system-on-chip with a combination of application core and real time core for housekeeping and low power operation. Here application core can be made to work on external PMIC while real time core can remain decoupled and rely on internal LDO providing a good combination of low power and fast response time with respect to wake-up from low power modes.

177

NOTE: *Most of the schemes shown in this section should be considered as examples rather than strict guidelines; however a System-on-Chip may have several restrictions that one may end up with a different combination of power scheme to meet target application needs.*

7.9 Power Management Examples

This section provides some application examples of power management in range of embedded devices.

7.9.1 Power Management for Wearables

One of the most common source of power in a wearable application like a Sports watch would be Chargeable Lithium-Ion battery as they can be designed to fit in any shapes required by the application. With an increasing trend to drive more graphics as watch no longer just displays time but other attributes like health information, Geo location driving current requirements drastically compared to typical digital watch. This pushes the need for DC-DC Converter to provide highest efficiency to increase battery life.

Figure 7-29 shows a power management scheme used on a typical sports watch [26] though not limited to.

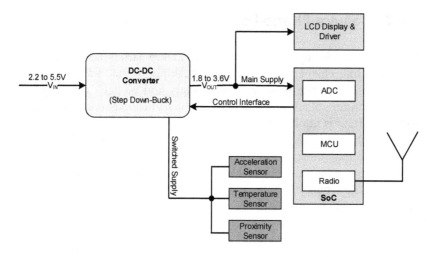

Figure 7-29: Power Management in a typical Sports Watch

Though LCD driver is shown separate, could be part of the same SoC though. Same applies for ADC and Radio. Need for small form factor would eventually push all these components to be part of same SoC in future [Except LCD Display].

A need for wider range of input voltage be supported by DC-DC would be necessary. Min voltage will be dictated by optimal point of battery voltage where voltage starts to drop drastically [typically in range of 2.2 to 2.4V] while upper limit would be limited by whether application need to allow operation from a USB Port [Typical for a sports watch] and thin-film solar modules.

DC/DC step-down based power management will enable ultra-low-power applications like a sports watch. A typical sports watch would atleast include few sensors like an accelerometer, Proximity sensor, temperature sensor etc., control for which may or may not be part of SoC. If there are several sensors that application has to deal with periodically waking up the system, another low power approach would be include another smaller SoC that just deals with sensors rather than main SoC to that is to be kept ON to manage the sensors. With a need for smaller form-factor, a dual core single chip would be another option where one core manages all the sensors while other core manages everything else. These are all the tradeoff that will dictate power scheme based on what application needs versus the cost of the overall solution.

7.9.2 Cellular Phone Power Management

Most phones today operate on a single cell Li-Ion battery, which has a 4.2V maximum fully charged voltage. If the cellular phone manufacturer requires the phone to operate with removed battery and plugged in charger the maximum input voltage of the system can be higher, depending on how the battery charger is implemented. In the past, the voltage regulator function was implemented using discrete low dropout linear regulators, LDOs however today most phones are built using more integrated power management solutions, that include a large number of regulators, LDOs and switching regulators, battery chargers, sequencing circuitry, supervisory and house-keeping circuitry [27].

Figure 7-30 shows an example for generic Power management IC for CDMA cellular phones.

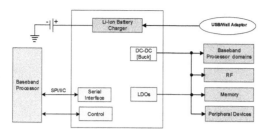

Figure 7-30 : Power management in a typical CDMA Cellar phone

The example shows Power Management IC to include a fully integrated Li-Ion battery charger with power FET and over-voltage protection, one Buck regulator and several low noise LDOs and a serial interface to program on/off conditions and output voltages of individual regulators and to read status information the Power Management IC.

The Li-Ion charger can safely charge and maintain a single cell Li-Ion battery operating from an AC adapter. Some chargers would often integrate a power FET with a thermally regulated charging to provide efficient charging rate for a given ambient temperature.

Some Buck regulators will also include an automatic switch to Pulse Frequency Modulation mode at low load conditions to provide good efficiency at low output currents.

7.9.3 Power Management for Tablets

High Power efficiency is one of the key requirements for Tablets to enable longer numbers of hours of operation in a single charge.

Figure 7-31 shows a custom PMIC (MC34708) designed especially to work as a companion IC with Freescale i.MX processor families.

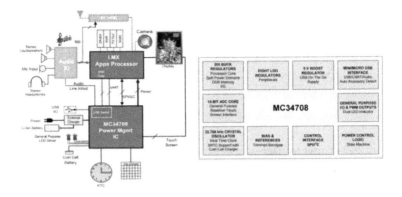

Figure 7-31: Power Management IC (MC34708) for Tablets[10] [28]

The MC34708 Power Management Integrated Circuit (PMIC) represents a complete system power solution in a single package. The MC34708 integrates six multi-mode buck regulators and eight LDO regulators for direct supply of the processor core, memory and peripherals.

Buck Regulators are specifically useful for high current load blocks. For example separate Buck regulator output can be dedicated for each processor core and memory island for different power domains. The USB switch enables the use of a single, mini or micro USB connector for USB, UART and audio connections, switching the relevant signals to the connector depending on the type of device connected. In addition, the MC34708 also integrates a real time clock, coin cell charger, a 13-channel 10-bit ADC, 5V USB Boost regulator, two PWM outputs, touch-screen interface, status LED drivers and four GPIOs [28].

7.9.4 Energy Harvesting

Ambient energy sources can be broadly divided into direct current (DC) sources and alternating current (AC) sources. DC sources include harvesting energy from sources that vary very slowly with time, such as light intensity and thermal gradients using solar panels and thermoelectric generators respectively [29]. The output voltage of these harvesters does not have to be rectified.

---

[10] Copyright Freescale Semiconductors (http://freescale.com). Used by Permission

AC harvesters include energy harvesting from vibrations and radio frequency power using piezoelectric materials, electromagnetic generators and rectifying antennae. The output of these energy harvesters must be rectified to a DC voltage before it can be used to power a system. In this section, only DC energy harvesters are considered as energy harvesters using these sources are easier to obtain in high volume quantities as opposed to AC harvesters [29].

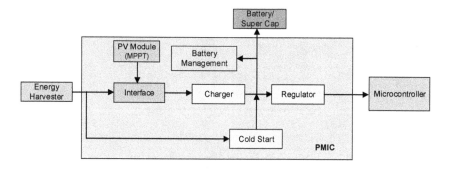

Figure 7-32: Generalized energy harvesting System [29]

Figure 7-32 shows a generalized architecture of an energy-harvesting system. The overall system consists of the ambient energy source, energy buffer (super capacitor/battery), the PMIC, and the system load. Since the energy available from the energy source is dependent on time-varying ambient conditions, the energy from the source is extracted when available and stored on the energy buffer. The system load is powered from the energy buffer. This allows the system to work, even if there is no ambient energy available. The power management unit itself consists of a DC/DC power converter with an optimized interface to the energy harvester, battery management circuitry, output regulator, and cold start unit.

The function of the *"Charger"* is to extract maximum possible energy from solar panel and transfer the energy to a storage element. The common charger topologies include linear dropout (LDO) regulators, buck converters, boost converters and buck-boost converters. For a solar panel, the topology is primarily dependent on the output voltage of the solar panel stack. Typically, the output of a single cell solar panel is 0.5V. Therefore, for systems with single cell and two cell solar panels, a boost converter topology is required, as battery voltages are typically greater than 1.2V for NiMH and 3V for Li-Ion batteries. For a higher number of series-connected cells, other converters such as a diode rectifier, buck regulator, or an LDO can be used.

To extract the maximum power from a solar panel, the panel must be operated at its maximum power point. A solar panel can be modeled as a reverse-biased diode that delivers current in parallel with a parasitic capacitance (C). The current output of the diode is proportional to the light intensity.

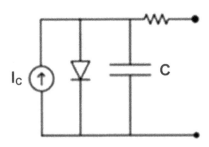

Figure 7-33: Model of a Solar Panel [29]

For a solar panel, the maximum power is obtained at approximately 80 percent of the open circuit voltage (OCV) [29]. The maximum power extraction circuit dynamically adjusts the input impedance of the power converter to extract the maximum power. For solar-energy harvesting, maximum power extraction is done using simple techniques such as input-voltage regulation at a fixed fraction of the open-circuit voltage, input-current regulation at a fixed fraction of the short-circuit current, or using complex microprocessor-based techniques.

Note that the choice of converter topology is a tradeoff between design complexity, component count, and efficiency. Switching converters typically provide better efficiency than linear regulators, but at the cost of increased components, design complexity and board space.

In energy-harvesting systems, an energy buffer is used to store the intermittently energy available from the energy harvester. The stored energy is then used to power the system. This architecture allows the overall system to operate continuously, even though the energy available is intermittent. The commonly used energy buffers include rechargeable batteries of different chemistries, as well as super capacitors.

The design considerations of the battery-management section are dependent on the energy buffer used. For rechargeable batteries, the OV and UV thresholds are based on the cell chemistry. For super capacitors, the OV and UV thresholds are determined by the lower value of the absolute max ratings of the IC and the capacitor. Using the optimal settings for the energy buffer maximizes the life time of the system.

Another consideration in the design of the battery-management section is the quiescent current consumed by the battery-management section. The circuitry in the battery-management block includes building blocks such as references, comparators, and digital logic. The current consumed by these circuits must be minimized. This is because any energy used by the battery-management section drains the battery and the energy is not being supplied to the external load.

The cold-start unit is an optional block that may or may not be present in a typical energy-harvesting PMIC. The function of the cold-start unit is to boot strap the system when there is insufficient energy stored in the storage element. The design of the cold-start unit is application dependent. For solar applications, an input-powered (as opposed to a battery-powered) oscillator can be used to drive the switches of a temporary low efficiency switching converter. Once sufficient energy has been built up in the energy buffer, the highly efficient switching converter can take over [29].

Finally the function of the regulator is to provide a regulated voltage from the battery. The topology of this block is dependent on the battery, system-load requirements, and quiescent current.

8. References

[1] W. Wolf, Computers as Components: Principles of Embedded Computing Systems Design, Elsevier, 2000..

[2] J. W. Valvano, Introduction to Embedded Microcomputer Systems, Motorola 6811 and 6812 Simulation, (International Student Edition), Thomson Learning, 2003.

[3] T. D. Morton, Embedded Microcontrollers, Pearson Education, 2001.

[4] AN1057, Selecting the Right Microcontroller Unit, Freescale Semiconductor, 2004.

[5] http://en.wikipedia.org/wiki/Harvard_architecture.

[6] K. Kant, Computer based Industrial Control, books.google.com (PHI Learning), May 2010.

[7] J. Groopman, Interoperability: The Challenge Facing the Internet of Things, 2013.

[8] G. Muller, Opportunities and Challenges in embedded systems, Buskerud University College, 2012.

[9] Wikipedia, "Vectored Interrupts, Wikipedia.org," [Online]. Available: http://en.wikipedia.org/wiki/Vectored_Interrupt.

[10] R. P. I. Manuel Jiménez, Introduction to Embedded Systems: Using Microcontrollers and the MSP430, Springer, 2014.

[11] M. ROMANCA, Interrupts and Exceptions, TRANSILVANIA University of Brasov.

[12] DSPIC33F Family Reference Manual Rev C, Micron Technologies, 2007.

[13] J. Yiu, *A Beginner's Guide on Interrupt Latency - and Interrupt Latency of the ARM® Cortex®-M processors*, ARMConnected Community, Sept 13, 2003.

[14] J. V. a. R. Yerraballi, Embedded Systems- Shape the world, e-book on utexas.edu.

[15] First Steps with Embedded Systems, Ontario: Byte Craft Limited, November 2002.

[16] NXP LPC176x/5x User Manual, Rev 3.1, NXP, April 2014.

[17] M. A. a. V. Jain, *Understanding embedded-system-boot techniques*, eetimes, 2011.

[18] C. N. Notes, "Cisco Router Booting Process Explained," http://computernetworkingnotes.com/.

[19] R. T. M. A. Suhas Chakravarty, *Need a watchdog for improved system fault tolerance?*, eetimes, 2008.

[20] D. Campbell, *Meeting IEC 60730 Class B Compliance with the MC9S08AW60*, Freescale Semiconductor.

[21] Maxim, "An Introduction to Switch-Mode Power Supplies (Application note 4087)," Maxim Integrated .

[22] Maxim, *"Switch Bounce and Other Dirty Little Secrets", Application Note 287*, Maxim Integrated, Sept, 2010.

[23] H. Zhung, "Basic Concepts of linear regulator and switching mode power supplies, part one," eetimes, Aug, 2013.

[24] D. Bonyuet, "Choose The Right Switching Regulator," Electronicdesign.com, Sept 2013.

[25] Embien, "Embedded Systems Design – Power Supply Design," Embien Technology Blog.

[26] O. Datasheet, "TPS82740x 360nA IQ MicroSIPTM Step Down Converter Module for Low Power Applications (Rev. A)," Texas Instruments, June 2014.

[27] K. S. Thomas Szepesi, "Cell phone power management requires small regulators with fast response," eetimes, Feb 2002.

[28] Freescale, "MC34708, Power Management Integrated Circuit (PMIC) for i.MX50/53 Families," Freescale Semiconductor, Nov 2013.

[29] J. C. B. L.-S.-C. Karthik Kadirvel, "Power-management functions for energy harvesting," eetimes, Aug 2012.

[30] T. Instruments, MSP430G2x44 Mixed-Signal Microcontrollers Datasheet, Texas Instruments, 2014.

[31] W. Wolf, Computers as Components: Principles of Embedded Computing Systems Design, Elsevier, 2000.

[32] Brian Dipert, *Banish bad memories*, EDN, Nov, 2001.

[33] J. Ganssle, *Great Watchdog Timers For Embedded Systems*, The Ganssle Group, 2011.

[34] S. Taranovich, "Power management for wearables: Designer options," September 29, 2014 .

[35] T. Instruments, "LP3923 Cellular Phone Power Management Unit," Texas Instruments, May 2013.

Embedded System Design